PRAISE FOR

THE NANNY CHRONICLES OF HOLLYWOOD

• •

Many years ago, when I first moved to Los Angeles, I remember calling my mum and saying, "Mum, things that happen in the movies happen in real life here!"

Having been a high-profile nanny in Hollywood, I found myself nodding as I turned the pages of *The Nanny Chronicles of Hollywood*. It was so fun to read, not only because I could relate, but because I loved seeing how Julie and Stella wove these somewhat eye-opening stories with a good measure of amusement yet also with neutrality. I think we could all learn a little about not taking ourselves quite so seriously from this book, as parents and as humans.

—Emma Jenner, author of *Keep Calm and Parent On*,
parenting coach, and founder of Emma's Children

Stella knows *exactly* what happens behind the gates and hedges of Hollywood. And if you want to know, too, you will have to buy this incredible book. It's a must-read even for us—and we lived it!

—Suzy Shuster, American broadcaster
and Emmy Award–winning sportscaster

The Nanny Chronicles of Hollywood is written in perfect, tangy, tart, tongue-in-cheek style by Stella Reid and Julie Swales. You never know what you might pick up by picking up this book.

—Rich Eisen, American TV journalist/sportscaster
and TV/radio host

"You can steal my husband, wreck my Beemer, and scuff my Birkin, but if you come anywhere near my nanny, I'll scratch your eyes out."

When a real—in the non-TV sense—Beverly Hills house-wife made this statement to me a few years ago, there were no signs of humor there. The eyes were fixed, the mouth curled into an angry snarl. Only later did I understand why: she was one of the many loyal fans of British nanny to the stars, Stella Reid.

In the senseless LA world of hypoallergenic grass lawns, parenting fads, and all-consuming neuroses, it takes home-grown Brits to prick the bubble. What Stella and her part-ner, Julie Swales, have witnessed defies belief: think *The Devil Wears Prada* set in the one-percentile world of child rearing, where nurseries are kitted out with $20,000 artworks, crystal-studded baby bathtubs, cashmere blankets of every conceiv-able color, and $1,300 designer children's coats.

— Celia Walden, US Editor-at-Large, *Daily Telegraph*

As a full-time working mother in the entertainment industry, I can say without question that there is no more important, or more complex, relationship than the one between a parent and her child's caregiver.

Author Julie Swales is a master at her craft, making sense of the nonsensical and helping mothers (and nannies) navigate through the uncharted and difficult dynamics they find themselves in. This book is a hilarious, touching, and all-too-informative *must*-read for moms everywhere!

—Marissa Devins, TV and literary agent

As a professional nanny consultant providing support for high-profile families all over the world, I have seen my own share of the challenges of working with a Hollywood family. There is a special set of rules for these very special people!

The Nanny Chronicles of Hollywood does a great job of capturing the antics of both nannies and families in the Hollywood world.

—Lindsay Heller, PsyD, The Nanny Doctor:
Consulting Services for Families and Nannies

While many of the relationships that are forged between nannies and the families they work for are of the most precious variety, some of them, well . . . not so much. And oftentimes when they are of the latter sort, the stories that are told by the nannies are far too outlandish to ever have been made up. Enter *The Nanny Chronicles of Hollywood*, a peek into the lives of those who care for the offspring of the world's most rich and famous and those who are auditioning for this most important part. You'll be pulled into a world that you never could have imagined really existed—and one you're left desiring to read more about.

—Michelle LaRowe, 2004 International Nanny Association Nanny of the Year, author of *Nanny to the Rescue!* and *Nanny to the Rescue Again!*

THE NANNY CHRONICLES OF HOLLY-WOOD

THE NANNY CHRONICLES OF HOLLY-WOOD

JULIE SWALES and STELLA REID

Published by Paisley Press

Edited and Designed by Girl Friday Productions
www.girlfridayproductions.com

Editorial: Jenna Land Free and Kristin Mehus-Roe
Cover and Interior Design: Paul Barrett

ISBN-13: 9780692421765
ISBN-10: 0692421769
Library of Congress Control Number is available.

First Edition

Printed in the United States of America

Because children have been at the center of our lives for decades, we decided to use this book as a platform to support them.

We are thrilled to partner with the Jacaranda Foundation (jacarandafoundation.org), which operates the Jacaranda School for Orphans in Malawi. The school was founded by Marie Da Silva, who was born and raised in Malawi and worked as a nanny in the United States for nineteen years.

This school is the only entirely free primary and secondary school in the whole of Malawi. They also operate an outreach program called malawiReads: Libraries & Literacy, which helps public primary and secondary schools set up their own libraries and build community libraries that offer free literacy classes.

For every copy of *The Nanny Chronicles of Hollywood* that is sold, we are providing a children's book to the Jacaranda Foundation. Please help us help these amazing children.

—Julie and Stella

CONTENTS

· · · · · · · · · · · · · · · · · · · ·

FOREWORD *1*

INTRODUCTION: WELCOME TO NANNYWOOD
From Downton to Nannywood *3*

CHAPTER ONE: THE INTERVIEW
*On Tightrope Walking and Other Feats
of the Would-be Nanny* *19*

CHAPTER TWO: THE CHARGES
*On RIE, Orgasmic Childbirth,
and Winston Churchill's Boyhood* *51*

CHAPTER THREE: THE SEX
And Throw in Some Sensibility, Too *83*

CHAPTER FOUR: THE LUXURY
Nanny Wears Prada. *121*

CHAPTER FIVE: BOUNDARIES
*Saying "Yes" and Meaning "No, Hell No,
Absolutely No!"*. *155*

CHAPTER SIX: THE BREAKUP
    The Breakup – On Graceful Departures
    and Nasty See Yas! *183*

CHAPTER SEVEN: THE REBIRTH
    What Nannies Have in Common with Butterflies . . . *211*

ACKNOWLEDGMENTS *225*

FOREWORD

· · · · · · · · · · · · · · · · · · · ·

Finding a nanny was definitely the hardest job I have ever had. In a perfect world I would stay home with my children, but as an actress that's not possible. When we started looking for a nanny, I had absolutely no clue where to begin. I was completely overwhelmed. And then I met Julie, who took the time to get to know me and my family. To her, finding our nanny wasn't just filling a position, it was completing our family.

In the end, Julie found me the most amazing nanny—and five years later she is still with us. If it were not for Julie, I do not know how I would be able to leave my house and go to work. A caregiver is truly the most intimate position, and, thanks to Julie, my kids have an even better nanny than Mary Poppins! Stella and Julie understand nannies and their families in a way no one else does.

The Nanny Chronicles of Hollywood is a great read. It is funny, edgy, and quite a page-turner. I particularly enjoyed following each of the composite stories and seeing how their personal journeys within their nanny positions turned out. Stella and Julie have collected their many years of experience into one fascinating, touching, and sometimes heartbreaking book.

Sarah Michelle Gellar
Actress and Producer

INTRODUCTION

· · · · · · · · · · · · · · · · · · · ·

Welcome to Nannywood

From Downton to Nannywood

In the United Kingdom, the nanny profession is a lofty one. It is considered one of the highest, greatest forms of service. Young women and men who aspire to be nannies—or mannies—can go to well-respected schools like Norland College, founded by Emily Ward in 1892. Norland College offers undergraduate degrees in Early Years Development and Learning, and graduates are highly sought after across the globe. Nannies are individuals who take care of children and nurture the next generation. How much more important can a job be? Not that our point needs proving, but it's worth mentioning that when she was nineteen, Lady Di was a nanny.

In the United States, we tend not to raise childcare providers. Just as teachers here are undervalued, so, too, are nannies. Here, the nanny position is sometimes considered one of domestic servitude. British nannies who move from the UK to the States are often perplexed at how US nannies seem to be almost apologetic about their job. Why lie and say you're a flight attendant, or a teacher, when you're really a nanny? What's wrong with being a nanny? In many parts of America, nannies are paid so little that it's not even considered a living wage. (Even Lady Di's pedigree didn't exempt her from this; when she worked as a nanny for an American family living in London, she earned just five dollars per hour.)

Many nannies in America are quite young, and often see nannying as a transitional job. It's something to do while they look for a "real job." Or they're not a legal resident, and need a job where they can be paid under the table. Or they aren't educated, and need a job that doesn't require a college— or even high school—degree. But mostly, it's something in between an education and a job—not a career.

So where does this all lead the bright, young, college-educated American who doesn't want to be a teacher, and yet wants to work with children? The individual who doesn't ever want a desk job, and who has had a wonderful way with kids since she babysat as a preteen?

It leads her to Hollywood, of course, where even if the role still isn't valued as it should be, at least it's well compensated.

Consider the plight of the Hollywood nanny. She may have taken a job far from home, and certainly one that routinely takes her far from home. She works long and irregular hours, rarely sees her friends or family, and finds it nearly impossible to date or form a life or identity of her own. She must love and invest in the children in her charge, but not grow so attached that they prefer her to their mum or that it hurts too much when she leaves her post. She must navigate household politics such as the imperiousness of the estate managers or personal assistants and the petty jealousies of housekeepers. She must navigate the sexual politics—looking presentable enough to keep up the family's appearances, but not so attractive she distracts from mum. She must be good at what she does, but not so good that other families want to poach her.

Let's now consider the plight of the Hollywood family. All eyes are on them, and often their careers depend on that spotlight. All eyes are also on their children: what they're wearing, what they're doing, whether mum and dad are ruining them so badly they'll be in rehab by their sweet sixteen. All eyes are also on mum and dad as they navigate through their cutthroat business. In Hollywood you're only as hot as your most recent movie or love interest. You're expected to keep up your former childless lifestyle, even after the little ones arrive. In short, there's the appearance of your life, and then there's your actual life.

At the highly charged intersection of these two worlds, you'll run across, well, us!

JULIE: I'm the director of the childcare division of the Elizabeth Rose Agency, the most prestigious staffing agency in Hollywood. I've placed nannies with the likes of Tom Cruise, Britney Spears, and Neil Patrick Harris. On any given day, I field phone calls from tearful mums who need some help and sanity in their lives and traumatized good-girl nannies who've discovered their new bosses were in the habit of wandering around the property naked.

STELLA: I'm the costar of the television series *Nanny 911*, and a successful Hollywood nanny and parenting coach. I know the awkwardness that arises when a child runs to the nanny—not the mum—for a kiss after an injury, and how lovely it is to travel in private planes after a lifetime of traveling coach. I also know the importance of keeping firm boundaries, and realizing when it's time to say good-bye and return to your own life.

The two of us have been friends for years, and some say our closeness is on account of our shared British heritage (Julie is from London, and Stella's from Lancashire), but it's more than that. In an industry where you must always be careful what you say and to whom, we found with one another we could be very direct and honest about the crazy world around us.

Picture the two of us drinking tea, eating chocolate biscuits, and dissecting yet another day of nanny drama.

One of us said, "Oh my God, if only people knew." Two hours and at least sixteen hilarious stories later, *The Nanny Chronicles of Hollywood* was born. We thought, let's give the Hollywood-obsessed public a peek into our decades of experience with Crazywood. We'll add parents, kids, and nannies to the mix, and see if something fun shows up.

Planning began, nanny interviews were scheduled and taped, stories were collected, and we suddenly realized we had enough information for *three* books. *And* a miniseries!

Between the two of us, we've worked in the business nearly forty years. We've lived a lot, and we've seen a lot. And while much of what we've observed transpired in the rarified air of Hollywood, we found that many observations were true outside of the childcare field, *and* outside of Hollywood.

We're going to share with you a behind-the-scenes tour of all the glamour, insanity, and heartwarming truths of the life of a Hollywood nanny. Four nannies' narratives (although, technically, one is a *manny*[1]) weave throughout the book, allowing you to witness their varied experiences, their growth, and the very different types of families they work for. Though names and identifying details have been changed and we've employed a composite strategy to protect the integrity of confidentiality agreements and the innocent, our stories and the stories of the nannies in this book are all

---

1   Note that wherever in the book we use the pronoun "she," we intend it to be interchangeable with "he."

true. We think you'll agree that some are hilarious in their outrageousness, some are touching, but all are fascinating.

Americans are truly celebrity crazy. You only have to drive down Sunset Boulevard on any given day to see open-topped tour buses stuffed to the gills with star-gazing tourists. The buses cruise popular lunch haunts, grocery stores, and coffee shops, all in hopes of catching a glimpse of someone who may be someone. If all else fails, they line up outside celebrity homes taking pictures of anyone arriving or leaving, including the staff. At least they work for someone who's someone, right?

What these fans don't know is famous celebs are just like us. Really, they are! But we don't *want* to know that, do we? We *want* to believe they are richer, shinier, and more beautiful versions of ourselves. And we want to believe they are all living the lives that for us would lead to the happiness we strive for. We believe they are who we want to be.

It's shocking to think that Lindsay Lohan or Paris Hilton being released from Lynwood jail will elicit more news coverage than looming Middle Eastern nuclear tensions, world elections, or trade deficit figures. We would rather pore over glossy magazines full of bad advertisements for lip fillers, or the latest lambskin ("you'll never know he's wearing it!") condom. We want magazines chock-full of celebrity gossip, and pictures of beautiful people in beautiful clothes. If only we could afford those styles, we might look like celebrities ourselves. Tabloid magazines hold the greatest share of real estate on supermarket shelves, and the industry is worth billions. And even those of you who profess not to buy them, you still read them in the nail salon! Are we obsessed, or are we obsessed?

Hollywood is a magnifier. Everything is *big* here—from the names, to the homes, to the cars, to the egos. That doesn't mean that other people don't experience the same interpersonal conflicts, but it's amplified in Hollywood. The celebrity nanny industry borders on the fantastical, and not always in a bad way. There are perks, you see, for putting up with the madness. We know heaps of nannies whose weddings have been hosted by their employers. We know of a nanny whose former charges, now adults, flew from around the world to be with her as she was dying. We know of nannies who still vacation with their former employers, only they bring their own kids along so everyone can play together. One employer bought a house for a nanny who had dedicated years of service to the family. At its best, the nanny-family relationship is a beautiful, unique, and strong bond that reminds us of our capacity for love and generosity. At its worst, it shines a light on the issues of power, class, and manipulation that come to the surface when one person is paid to care for another's children. Throw the narcissistic and materialistic culture of Hollywood into the mix, and all these themes are amplified.

So let's start with the first stop on our behind-the-scenes tour: the nanny agency. For this portion of our program, Julie will be your guide.

Parents use different approaches when looking for a nanny. Some will spend hours trolling through Craigslist or online nanny databases looking for their perfect Mary Poppins. This is inexpensive, but can be a lengthy process and quite stressful for a mum who is new to the nanny arena and soon to be headed back to work. Really, it's like dating. Would you date someone you met on Craigslist, or go ahead and pay for eHarmony?

Enter stage left: the nanny placement agency. These agencies, if run well, take the pain out of the process for busy parents. All the mum—or a member of her staff—needs to do is contact an agency and within an hour they will receive an e-mail with a selection of prescreened considerations. Once trials are complete and a nanny is chosen, all financial offers are handled by the agency, which is a huge support. Then, as the relationship between the family and nanny moves forward, the agency can act as a mediator and sounding board when things go a little awry, which, as with all relationships, they're bound to at some point.

Just as nannies are screened for clients, clients are also screened. If a family wants someone to work sixty-plus hours a week for a pittance, they'll be hard-pressed to find a reputable agency to work with them. Nanny agencies also make sure nannies have work agreements where hours, pay, and annual vacations are listed. A good agency will stand up for the nanny's rights when disgruntled employers feel that sacking the nanny without severance is acceptable.

Ah, but there's another, sneakier way some parents find good nannies: they poach them from their friends! We love the observations of Celia Walden, a journalist for the *Telegraph*, who has the perfect summation of the inner workings of Hollywood from a mum's perspective. If you have a stellar nanny, she writes, keep her close. A good nanny is hard to find, and there are many who will try to woo her from you. To avoid her appearing too attractive to other mums, Celia writes, play down her good points, "and get inventive about her bad ones. Every time 'vulture mum' at the school gates mentions how sweet your help is, nod and add distractedly, 'Of course, it's a relief that she's pretty much got the facial herpes under control.' If that doesn't do it, a strategically placed anecdote about the time you came home early to find her trying on your Alaïa pumps ('I wouldn't mind, but what with her size-41 feet they're all stretched out') should work just as efficiently" ("Celia Walden Keeps Her Eyes Peeled for the Nanny-Nabbers of Beverly Hills," November 20, 2014).

But assuming that incidences of poaching are few and far between, the agency is the route of choice for most families.

At Elizabeth Rose, each nanny is vetted very carefully—much more carefully, in fact, than some presidential running mates. In addition to interviewing them extensively, we look through their online presence—including Instagram, Facebook, Pinterest, Twitter, Tumblr, Google, and LinkedIn. Never before have our personal lives so blended with our professional and public lives. In the world of Hollywood domestic employment, that blend can be an utter disaster. If a nanny wants to be at the top of the pyramid, she must make every effort to erase anything that might stand in her way.

In addition to closely reviewing their presence on social media, we also chat with their previous employers and run extensive criminal background checks. If a prospective nanny makes it to the final stages, we give her thorough instructions regarding her attire for her interview. Some nannies have had sales assistants at the Gap or Banana Republic send us photos of the candidate wearing different outfits, and we'll pick one out for them. Then we begin to contemplate which family would make the best fit.

COMMON SENSE IS NOT VERY COMMON

Whether she realizes it or not, a nanny's first interview begins the moment she steps into the nanny agency. Just because she has a padded-out résumé doesn't mean she doesn't need to work the nanny agency crowd. One thing that drives Julie crazy is when nannies who have been working for five or six years act as if they know everything about the profession. Unless they've been a nanny for five or six years *in Hollywood*, they are beginners. Some of the worst judgment calls we've seen:

1. Long garish fake nails.
2. A shirt short enough and pants low enough to reveal a tramp stamp.
3. Six-inch stilettos and an outfit fit more for a club than a nanny agency interview.
4. Excessive cleavage.
5. So much perfume she overpowers the room.

But believe it or not, Julie does not necessarily send these candidates packing. Common sense is not common, but it can be taught. If a candidate has a sparkle in her eye, a Mary Poppins magic, a light when she talks about children, and a willingness to be molded, Julie is prepared to mold. She's happy to be Henry Higgins to their Eliza Doolittle.

"Are you willing to completely reinvent yourself for a celebrity position?" she asks.

If they get excited and say, "What do you want me to do?" they're in.

When a client calls Julie to request a nanny, it's most often the mum. The first questions Julie asks her are "What is it you need in your life? What roles do you need filled? What's going to make you sleep better at night?" More often than not, she needs another her. She needs a wife.

For Julie, this is when the fun really begins. This is when the matchmaking starts. Stella calls her a "domestic architect."

Julie is asked all the time how she chooses which candidates to recommend to which families. Perhaps someday she'll take a few years off and chart it all, to see if there are clear variables and patterns. But her suspicion is that there isn't reason to it at all—only a bit of art, and a strong spoonful of intuition. How else can you explain her knowing that the dreadlocked, tattooed, nose-ringed nanny has the perfect energy for the anxiety-ridden mother of two? Or that the Latina girl who had a run of bad luck and even lived out of her car for a time has an authenticity that will be appreciated by some of Julie's down-to-earth clients? Or how the very feminine lesbian is somehow the perfect fit for the gay dads raising three sons? Okay, so that one should seem obvious.

But the match really is only the beginning. Once they've got past the agency interview and the background screening, then they must get past the house manager, personal assistant, then the parents, then the children, then the trial period.

We've structured this book so that you can see the different stages of the nanny's life. Just as the butterfly begins as an egg, then becomes a larva, and then a pupa before changing into its final, glorious winged form, the Hollywood nanny, too, must go through several stages before she is fully evolved. She must learn to manage the privileged children, who might often resemble Veruca Salt and are not fond of the word "no." She must learn to maneuver through a sometimes sexually charged environment, and must also learn that all that glitters is not gold. Most importantly, she must learn to set clear boundaries before she can be free. And then she must start all over again.

THE HOUSEHOLD HIERARCHY

When you see a celebrity, you often see him with an entourage. There's also a behind-the-scenes entourage that keeps his life running smoothly. Many wealthy households will keep a full domestic staff, and within that staff there is very clear hierarchy. Heaven help the nanny who loses sight of her position! The rankings are as follows:

1. **The Business Manager:** If the house manager holds the keys to the kingdom, the business manager holds the keys to the pocketbook, and holds them tight! Business managers hover over every cent of their clients' the way a parent hovers over a teenager with her first checkbook or bank account.

2. **The House Manager:** This is the boss, the person who creates the schedules, gives performance reviews, and holds the keys to the kingdom.

3. **The Personal Assistant:** This is the person who is there 24-7 for whatever the celebrity needs, be it a pencil or a gluten-free cracker. They function like living, breathing versions of Siri.

4. **The Butler:** The butler represents the family from the moment he opens the front door. He is the face of the household, the maître d' of social events, and the manny to the man of the house.

5. **The Governess:** No, this is not your average nanny. She is an accredited educator.

6. **The Baby Nurse:** This is a highly paid and highly respected position. Temporary as it may be, she's the gatekeeper to the new infant. If you're trying to organize a bris, good luck getting past the baby nurse!

7. **The Nanny:** The nanny is the subject of this book. You'll know her pretty well by its end!

8. **The Chef:** A very respectable career, and often a difficult one, given the range of dietary restrictions these days (dad's Paleo; mum's vegan; kids are carbs, carbs, carbs; and the nanny's juicing).

9. **The Estate Manager's Assistant:** Think car washing, light-bulb changing, patio cleaning, doubling up as a waiter during dinner parties, and Barbie-house building.

10. **The Security Detail:** Some families have as many as ten people who work security, and often they're armed.

11. **The Driver:** While many celebrities like to drive themselves in their fancy sports cars, drivers are also always on payroll. These drivers must be able to dodge the paparazzi,

evade undesirables, and be able to beat the traffic like a Hackney carriage driver who passed the Knowledge test.[2]

12. **The Housekeeper and Laundress:** They are qualified in the art of all things eco-friendly and all things gossip-related.

13. **The Gardener:** The head gardener is an educated horticulturalist, who is often in charge of an entire landscaping crew. This crew ranges from patio scrubbers to in-house floral arrangers. (When the crew isn't busy in the garden, they're getting busy with the housekeepers.)

2   To be an accredited taxi driver in London, you must first pass a test showing you've memorized the city's 25,000 streets and can find your way easily around them at any time of day. It takes years of study, so take that, GPS!

CHAPTER ONE

· · · · · · · · · · · · · · · · · · · ·

The Interview

On Tightrope Walking and Other Feats
of the Would-Be Nanny

As you observe what it's like for a nanny, forget everything you think you know about interviewing for a job. This is not Fleet Street, Wall Street, Main Street, or Sesame Street. This is not a street at all, but a boulevard—Hollywood Boulevard, to be exact—where rules apply, to be sure, just not the ones you think.

Even trickier, there is not one set of rules for Hollywood families—in this case, one size does not fit all. Until you figure out what a particular family's rules are, the most effective course is to be a blank slate. Think *Mary Poppins*, where an endless line of identical, darkly clad nannies carrying the exact same black umbrella line up to be interviewed by Mr. Banks. This is what the Hollywood nanny aims for: to blend in with the pack. The end goal here is to be as inoffensive as possible in a landscape where "offensive" is a constantly moving target.

Remember, parents are often looking for reasons *not* to hire someone rather than to hire her. They're looking for her problems, you see. They want to know how their decision to hire her might backfire on them. If a nanny is new to town, they're going to worry she'll get lost driving the kids to their various playdates and activities. If she has an amazing résumé, they'll worry that she's not there for the long term and that eventually she'll leave to get a "proper" job. If she doesn't have a wedding ring, they'll worry she is looking for a husband. If she does have a wedding ring, they'll worry that she's going to have a baby. If she doesn't have children of her own, they'll worry that she'll grow too attached to theirs. And if she does have children, they'll worry that she'll ask for time off every time her kids get sick.

But at the outset, the nanny has no idea what their particular set of worries are. It's a little bit as if she's a Michelin-star chef, who has all the skills to make an exquisite meal, but she knows it's best to wait and to listen to what the client wants before jumping into the kitchen. The recipe for a successful interview: plain clothes, plain hair, plain makeup, an authentic persona, and a good ear for listening.

NO CLOTHES, WILL TRAVEL

Meet Monique: tall, blond, fit, and French. When she interviewed with a famous Hollywood family, she was asked to walk around in a bikini before she was offered the job. Later she noticed that *all* the staff were tall, blond, and fit. The house manager said it was so that when the family and staff were lounging poolside in Bora-Bora or strolling the beach in Malibu, the press wouldn't know who was the family and who was the staff. Monique thinks they just liked beauty, but she took it as a compliment and worked for them for years.

Of course, we're not suggesting the nanny needs to hide her personality during an interview. But she shouldn't show so much of it that the family worries they'll be living with Jim Carrey. She must not be mute, and should be ready to take advantage of opportune moments to sell herself. She must never discuss money. (How gauche! That's why business managers and agents exist!) She must never, ever say anything disparaging about a previous employer, even if her previous employer was Cruella De Vil.

Lately we've seen more families take the stress interview approach. This is a tactic taken from the business world. It's used most commonly in headhunting when companies are hiring major CEOs and CFOs. The interviewers are negative and mean for the sole purpose of seeing how the candidate functions under stress. Sometimes one parent plays "bad cop" while the other plays "good cop." This being Hollywood, everybody knows each other, so sometimes they'll say negative things about the nanny's previous employers to see if she'll stick up for them, or they may say terrible things to the nanny to see if she'll stick up for herself. (And sticking up for herself may or may not be a good thing. She will only find out when the agency lets her know if she's made it to the next round.)

In addition to the parents, the Hollywood interview often includes important supporting players known as The Gatekeepers. Most often The Gatekeepers include business managers, house managers, and, occasionally, head nannies. But sometimes The Gatekeepers are less . . . conventional, and may include psychics or handwriting experts. We've actually seen parents have the nanny's chart done before they offer her an interview, because they simply can't hire a Scorpio. Then again, Scorpios *are* known to be stubborn and driven to succeed, so the parents might have a good reason to shy away.

Although Julie advises all nanny candidates that they don't have to answer personal questions that could violate employment law, some families ask them anyway. A nanny may be asked whether she is dating anyone, whether she plans to have children, or, especially in the case of a male nanny, whether he is gay.

"What did you think of Sarah?" Julie asked a family she'd been trying to match with a nanny for ages. She'd searched far and wide, and she'd finally found them the perfect nanny for their family—loads of experience, a charming but understated manner, flexible, and so right for this family that she even *looked* like them.

"You're right, Julie, she's perfect," the mum said. "Except we can't hire her."

"Why is that?" Julie asked, trying not to choke on her tea.

"She's been married for three years."

"Okay, and?"

The mum sighed. "Well, she told us she doesn't want to have kids until her college loans are paid off—somewhere around 2019—but you know, we really can't take the risk."

Julie wanted to remind her that it was only 2013 and she thought that six years was plenty of time. But she didn't press her. They were concerned Sarah would get pregnant and leave them. Another candidate crossed off, and it's back to the drawing board we go.

In the end, this family interviewed 132 nannies, tried out 30, shortlisted 8, and had all 8 work a week each. Then they put their search on hold.

Another family rivaled the difficulty of this one. After *ages and ages* of trying, Julie found them a perfect match. The family adored her, and Julie was sure they could finally hit the go button and sign a contract. And then at the eleventh hour, the parents saw the nanny's Pinterest boards. She had flagged some lingerie she liked. The nanny wasn't *wearing* the lingerie, just indicating her preferred style. But it was too risqué for the mum, who claimed she wouldn't be able to look at the nanny without imagining her in said lingerie. "We have access to too much information," the dad bemoaned. "I almost don't *want* to know the stuff I can learn. It's a wonder anyone gets a job."

No kidding, Julie thought as she went back to her files. It was frustrating, but really she blamed herself. There is someone at Elizabeth Rose whose sole job is to search for the nanny's online footprint. The agency had obviously dropped the ball.

It's not that the parents don't expect their nannies to have interests. But they want the nanny to be very, very clear that taking this job means giving up a lot of her life. What parents want to hear is: "I have no life. My life is your life. I will not be taking time off work to attend music festivals or writers' conferences. I am yours." The parents feel like they pay for this kind of commitment—and they do.

This is where your two lovely authors have a difference of opinion about just how troubling this phenomenon is. To break it down, here's where we fall:

STELLA: If someone won't hire a nanny because she's got a life, it's bloody selfish.

JULIE: No. It's just *honest*! This is Hollywood. This is what they're paying for, for the nannies to put their lives second, and the family's life first. They are paying good money for childcare, much more money than a nanny could get anywhere else.

STELLA: I still say it's bloody selfish.

And so what can we do but leave you to make up your own mind on it!

Then there's the dance of the rejection, a phenomenon as equally befuddling as the interview to those outside Hollywood. We've had many a nanny call after an interview, convinced she got the job. "They loved me! I could tell! They even asked if I could start on Monday!"

"That's great!" Julie says. Then she calls the family to check in, only to find out that no, they didn't like the nanny at all. In their minds, the interview was horrid!

What accounts for the disparity of impressions? Well, remember, many of these people we work with act for a living. And if they can afford a high-caliber nanny, they've probably had some degree of success at it. They are very good at making the nanny like them, and making the nanny think they like her, because this is what they do. Add to that the nanny is in their home and thus knows where they live. (Big security risk.) It's not surprising they're as nice to the nanny as possible, give her the impression that she's got the job, and leave the unpleasantness to someone else! If you really stop and think about it, can you blame them?

All this is enough to make a would-be Hollywood nanny run for the hills, but amazingly most don't. "I don't put much stock in the interview process," one nanny explained. "I've had terrible interviews where the parents were really just testing me, but it wasn't how they were at all. And I've had interviews where the parents were super sweet—but within five minutes of trialing for them I saw that they were batshit crazy."

Which brings us to those first five minutes, or the beginning of what's known as a "trial." When a nanny gets past the interview, she will often be asked to do a trial for the family, which she'll be paid for even if she isn't ultimately offered the job. Of course, before the nanny starts the trial—and often even before her first interview—she must sign away her life to lawyers. She is being let into an inner sanctum, and she may only be there for a couple of weeks. She is, understandably, a risk. Given how we all love anything and everything celebrity, the families must protect themselves.

Usually, but not always, as much as they may try to hide them, a family's warts will come out during the trial period. We've had nannies call and beg to get out of a trial after just one day. Generally we tell them, "Stick it out—you can't really know after just one day!" Sure enough, the phone rings a few days later and the nanny is elated with the family. She has got over the hump and she would do anything to stay on. Occasionally the answer is "Okay, let's get you out." One nanny called, traumatized, because the family, as it turned out, were nudists. Not a deal breaker, unless you're a conservative Mormon, and don't want to gaze on your boss's Brazilian each morning. The stretch was clearly too much for her, and it wasn't productive for anyone to keep her there a moment longer.

One nanny thought her weekend live-in trial was going swimmingly well. Until she was awoken at three o'clock in the morning by security and, still wearing her pajamas, escorted off the premises. Another family used the trial to test the nanny's ethics. They offered her a drink, and then a toke on a pipe. Heaven help the nanny who accepts! The answer is always, always no. (Really, does this even bear mentioning? Common sense, people!)

TRIAL BY FIRE

A favorite nanny story of ours comes from Rachel, a twenty-nine-year-old from Scotland, whose trial period coincided with one of the family's many trips. Lucky for Rachel, she learned through her trial that a job with this family would put her on par with a pack mule:

On a Thursday I heard I had a trial and should be at the house the next day at ten o'clock for a few hours' training. En route to Beverly Hills Friday morning, I got a call from the agency asking if I had my suitcase with me, as we would be flying to Switzerland three days earlier than planned—at one o'clock that very day. I made a quick about-turn, ran around my apartment like a chicken with no head, and not long after that I drove through the gates of the mansion with suitcase and passport in hand. The butler ushered me into the house with a sense of urgency that told me these people meant business.

When we pulled up to the curb at LAX, mum grabbed the baby and walked off, dad looked in my direction and said, "Get the bags." I looked behind me, thinking he must be talking to the driver, but there was no one there. Surely he was kidding? He wasn't, and they weren't bags, they were effin' trunks. So there I was, feeling more like a bellhop than a professional nanny.

We landed in New York and got off to board a private plane to Switzerland. Awesome, I thought. No more bag carrying for me. Well, apparently the staff must have got the memo that Girl Friday was flying the skies, 'cause there I was again like a European pack mule, schlepping everyone's luggage onboard the plane.

When we arrived in Switzerland, I was exhausted and wondering what I'd signed up for. Walking down the steps of the plane I took a deep breath and told myself, "You can do this, girl." The parents were already off the plane and getting into the huge limo that was waiting on the tarmac. All of a sudden, dad started walking back toward me and I thought, "Wonderful! He's going to take one of these bags off my breaking shoulder." But he just grunted at me, "You need to put the car seat in, and please hurry up." I started to reply, "You know what, jerk-off, why don't you shove a brush up my arse and I'll sweep the runway as I go back and forth? In fact, why not just call me effin' Cinderella?" But I bit my tongue.

After a busy few days we were to leave for Rome. The morning of our intended departure, the baby was sleeping and the mum was reading a magazine. I asked if it was okay for me to pop down the street to pick up a dress for my niece. "Oh yes, of course. Go, I've got things covered here," the mum replied.

Two hours later, the dad came barging into my bedroom, no knock on the door, no polite "excuse me," and announced, "You took time to go shopping when you were on the clock. You are just not focused. This isn't going to work out." I took a deep breath, put my balled Scottish fist into my trouser pocket, and with all the poise I could muster, replied, "No, it isn't."

In addition to finding out whether the nanny and family click or not, the trial allows both to find out more about one another. Does the family follow the same general child-rearing philosophy as the nanny? Do the rest of the staff like their jobs? How much turnover is there? Are the children monsters, or do they seem capable of reforming? Do the parents micromanage or will they be entirely absent?

The interview and trial provide a nanny the opportunity to set limits, to assess if her boundaries will be respected, to explain that yes, she is a Scorpio, but wonders if your psychic is really the right person to be consulting with on a decision as important as *who will take care of your child*. But, truthfully, the typical nanny does not say or do any of this. She needs the job. She wants the job. She'll sort out the rest later, and then we'll see what she's really made of.

Once a nanny passes her interview and her trial, there comes another major moment: the negotiation. As with most business transactions, there are middlemen. Or middle-*women*. Julie most typically works with the business manager of the Hollywood family to determine the finer points of the salary, how and when the nanny will be paid, how much she will be expected to travel, and how she will be compensated when she goes beyond her contracted hours. Sometimes we work on such details as how to get the nanny's car and possessions moved out from Montana, or wherever she lives, so that she can be ready to start work within forty-eight hours.

While it's usually the business manager handling these negotiations, this is also where the dad may show interest in the process for the first time.

"Julie!" one irate Hollywood producer dad shouted into my phone one day. "How can I be expected to pay six figures for a nanny when I only pay production assistants $450 a week?!"

"It's simple," I said. "It's supply and demand. If your assistant leaves, there's a queue around the block of people willing to take her place. Meanwhile, your wife has seen thirty nannies and only likes two." Silence. Deal done!

Wondering how much a nanny is paid? A qualified nanny (by which we mean a teacher, someone with a preschool or child development background, or a college graduate who has nannied through school) who is just starting out in the field might make $65,000 a year, but can earn double and even triple that in time, depending on the family.

Most weeks when Julie is in deep conversations with a celebrity's business manager, at some point the manager will say, "Don't share any of this information with my staff. They don't get paid anywhere near this much, and I don't want them leaving to become a nanny."

When you break down the perks, it can look like this:

- Six-figure salary
- 401(k) matching
- Health benefits with dental and orthodontic and vision ($500/month)
- $3,000-a-month housing allowance
- New SUV to drive the children around in or a car allowance if you're using your own car
- Personal grocery allowance, up to $200/week
- Travel pay/per diem, around $150/day on top of your salary
- Allowance for specific clothes to wear while at work
- Bonuses, often up to $10,000 at Christmas, plus an annual raise of 10 percent

For now, if you're wondering why the hell you're not a nanny, well, it's a good question. Do read on.

First Flirtation

Just as anyone does when they step into a different workplace, nannies must adjust to an entirely new set of rules, philosophies, and habits—but because these jobs are so personal, so intimate, and because they involve children's lives, it is, well, *loaded*. Fraught. Intense. Important. It's like committing to marry someone, but in Hollywood terms, where marriages come and go. As they stand on the precipice, nannies know it will be hard to walk away even if the job's not working out. And will she even be able to see that it's not working out, or will she be blinded by her affection for the child or for the mum, or by the paycheck she now can't live without?

The interview is where it all begins. It's the initial flirtation. The trial is where it evolves. It's where everyone is typically on their best behavior. The negotiation is where it becomes real. And by then, she's in, all in. Then she gets to see what she has really signed up for. One nanny we know gave up her apartment and a good job in LA to live with a family in Australia—it wasn't a decision she took lightly, but she had trialed with them and loved them. And then guess what? Honeymoons end, and she was back stateside struggling to put it all back together. Because just as you can go out on several dates with a man and think he's great, it's not until the waitress on your tenth date spills water on him and he screams at her that you really see what he's made of. It works the other way, too. Sometimes the interview and trial don't feel completely right, but when the nanny takes the job she grows to understand that it is the job she was meant to have. While perhaps the attraction was not immediate, she has found the love of her life.

Now, let's enter the rarified world of three Hollywood nannies and one Hollywood manny, who have discovered for themselves the pitfalls and perils of the job.

KIRSTEN

*P*lease please please please let me get this job, I muttered. My rent's nearly due, and if I'm not careful my car might be repossessed. I know my résumé speaks for itself but I also know that I need to keep my finances and credit record strong, especially if I'm going to land a high-profile Hollywood job— it's one of the first pieces of documentation any employer will ask for. As my tires crunched on the circular gravel driveway I stifled a gasp as the house came into view. It was amazing. I felt as though I'd just driven up to a house as imposing as Downton Abbey, but instead of being smack in the middle of the English countryside, this house was smack on the beach in Malibu. And instead of a redbrick façade it was almost completely made of glass, and the sea sparkled through each window. I'd heard from the agency that the parents were charming, very approachable, and, most importantly, quite down-to-earth. I hadn't met them yet, but they were Hollywood A-listers, funny and witty in every article I'd read about them in *Vanity Fair*. A job of this caliber would propel me to the next level of nannydom—I'd have reached the highest echelon.

I'd had a slew of dud interviews lately for some pretty bleak jobs. I had one interview where I was sure the mom and I connected, but her psychic said no—my aura or something like that was all wrong. Then, on the very first day of my last trial, the house manager informed me that not only did the family have six dogs, but none of the dogs were house-trained. The beasts just let it go on the marble floors and plush oriental carpets whenever nature called. Part of my job was walking the six dogs several times a day, and picking up excrement each time I came across it in the house. I could work wonders with a tantrumming toddler, but three hundred pounds of dog on a leash? Constantly having to watch my step indoors or risk covering my shoes with shit? Forget it. I gritted my teeth and got through the day, but I called Julie the second I was done.

"Don't go back," she said.

"Won't it be a black mark on my name if I don't finish the trial?" I asked.

"This wasn't in the job description; it's not fair," she said. "That's on them, not you."

But we both knew walking away was a risk. Families get insulted if you leave even if it was their doing. They could spread stories about you to their friends, and, true or not, if no one would hire you, what did it matter? But I knew I would never take this job, and after just one day at the house, I doubt I'd even registered on the parents' radar. It was safer to leave right away. I was out.

Days had passed before Julie called with this interview. I'd had a couple of calls from other agencies trying to persuade me to take something more middle of the road. I was holding out, though, for my dream job, and I knew it would be worth it even if I had to spend my days gnawing my nails and looking for my car each morning in case it had been repo'd overnight.

I had to get this job. I smoothed my skirt, adjusted my button-down shirt. I looked like a Gap girl, just as Julie had advised. Colorful, a little preppy, professional but not, like, law-firm professional.

The house manager, Sasha, met me at the door. She was petite, attractive, with bobbed black hair and a crisp, clipped manner. "Kirsten? Come on in." She welcomed me into the grandest, most opulent entrance hall I'd ever seen. Marble columns reached up several stories high, and the floor was so polished that I swear it was reflecting the sunlight. As I'd suspected, floor-to-ceiling windows revealed the stunning ocean view just beyond the back steps. "Would you like some water? Sparkling or flat?"

"Thank you, I'm fine," I said. I knew better than to set myself up for a round of hiccups.

"The office is just in through here," she said, as we walked down a hallway that seemed to go on and on. Finally, we turned into a bright room that was both cozy and professional. The seat offered to me was beyond comfortable—think Restoration Hardware meets a cloud. The soft fabric melted around me. It was like someone had taken my dad's old La-Z-Boy, wrapped it in high class, and placed it gingerly in the middle of the ocean.

Sasha asked me the usual questions, the ones I'd answered at practically every interview I'd done since becoming a nanny, about how I handled difficult scenarios, my education, my family. She reminded me of the importance of discretion. Then she asked one that threw me. "How would you handle an environment with a lot of yelling? Would that bother you?"

I studied her face, looking for signs of apology or embarrassment. But she looked professional, stone-cold serious, although I did see her painted-on smile quiver at the corner, just a bit.

"Yelling between who?"

"Between the parents, mostly. But there's," she looked around to make sure we were alone, "some yelling at the kids and between the kids, too."

Red flag, red flag, red flag! Get out of here, Kirsten! I knew the true answer: "Well, I believe yelling conveys a lack of respect, and I don't think I could work anywhere where the people didn't show respect for one another. How could they respect *me*?" But that wasn't the *right* answer, so it wasn't what I said. The salary for this job was amazing, so if that meant tuning out some yelling, so be it. So I said, more or less honestly, "I think it would be jarring at first, but I could get used to it."

Sasha considered my answer, looked at me closely with an unreadable expression, her pained smile quivering again. She sighed and put down her notebook. "Wait here a moment."

She returned a minute later. "Normally, I would send you home and call you back for another interview with Tess and Ron," she said, referencing her bosses. "But they'll both be leaving for Cannes tomorrow, so if you don't meet them now, it might be a while before we have another opportunity. Please follow me."

She led me up a staircase and into a cozy sitting area, where Tess was sitting on the couch drinking a cup of tea. Her legs were tucked under her, and she was wearing leggings and a long cashmere sweater. She stood up when she saw me, her long blond hair looking like she'd just stepped away from a stylist chair; her body was like that of a twentysomething yoga teacher, and even without makeup she was the most beautiful person I had ever seen.

"Kirsten!" she said, walking over and giving me a warm handshake. "I've heard great things about you. Please, come sit down. Can I get you a cup of tea?"

I'd worked for celebrities before, and I'd worked for beautiful people before and I'd always prided myself on ambivalence about fame, but Tess rendered me starstruck, and moments like this made me realize I was kidding myself. Tess Gallant, *the* Tess Gallant, one of the most beautiful and recognizable faces in America, was offering to make me a cup of tea! We all know she wasn't going to make it herself but you get the idea. *Why yes, Tess, I would like a cup of tea! One sugar, please!* But I demurred.

"It's lovely to meet you," I said, sitting where she'd motioned to on the plush couch.

Ron came into the room and strode right over to me. "Kirsten," he nodded, and put out his hand. He smiled, showing off his well-known dimples, and I melted a little inside. *Kirsten, get control of yourself! Keep your head!* But really, what my head was saying was that Sasha had it all wrong—there was no way people this beautiful could yell at one another or their children.

We talked for almost an hour, and by the end of it, I was smitten. I had forgotten that I was even trying to keep my guard up. Tess confessed how stressful it was, always having to dodge cameras and make a plan to deal with paparazzi. Her blue eyes watered as she told me about the betrayal of some of their previous employees; that was the reason they'd had to insist on a lengthy confidentiality contract. Ron asked me questions about what I liked to do, who I spent time with, and if I liked to travel (I did!). It turned out we both loved surfing. Clearly this was meant to be!

When the interview was over they both hugged me, and nodded to Sasha, who had been standing by the door the whole time. As I followed Sasha down the staircase, and down the interminable hallway, I heard Tess shout that they were looking forward to seeing me again very soon.

"So, assuming we can work out a financial arrangement, could you start on Monday?" Sasha asked.

Monday? It was Friday now. It seemed odd that they needed someone so quickly. What happened to their previous nanny? Did they only like me because they were desperate, or was I really a good fit? I put all my fears aside.

"Absolutely!"

JEREMY

Are you wearing *that* to the interview?" my mom asked.

I looked down. Khakis and a button-down blue shirt. Not too tight. No tie. Loafers.

"Um, yes. Why?"

Mom smiled and shook her head. "You spilled something on your pants. Look."

I looked down at my thighs. Sure enough, there was a light splotch of something—milk from my cereal, maybe?

Crap. I ran back into my room and changed into another pair that, thank God, she'd ironed for me. Leave it to my mom to be perfectly irritating and indispensable at the same time.

I hated that I'd had to move back home. I'd always intended to be self-sufficient and on my own the moment I graduated from college. And it had worked, for a while. I'd gone east, and had loved my job working for the New York Public Schools. But when I lost my job, I had to choose between eating and paying the rent. Rent was nuts, and there wasn't any cushion to look for another job. Even if I'd found one, I wouldn't have been paid in time to keep my apartment. It made more sense to move home while I saved up for a rainy day—I now knew there would be rainy days.

It had been great being home, in a way. I knew my mom liked the company and the security of having another person in the house. And any money I earned I could save for grad school. When I first came home, I'd worked at a Fred Segal, but was approached one day by a dude who wanted to know if I knew any male nannies. He had three boys, and wanted a guy to look after them.

We got to talking about my background with kids, and I told him I was planning to study child psychology in grad school. Before I knew it, I had a job taking care of his kids. He was a big-shot producer, but not that recognizable. Still, it meant he could pay me twice as much as I earned at Fred Segal. A job in my field, with flexibility? And I got to pretty much throw water balloons around all day. It was perfect. But then something went south. I never knew what I did wrong, but the business manager came to me one day and told me the family wanted a female nanny after all. He said I'd get three weeks' severance and that I could use his name to get another job. And that was that.

I was thinking about going back to Fred Segal, but the business manager unexpectedly called me a few days later. "I was talking to a friend who's on Mr. Black's staff," he said.

"The director? *That* Mr. Black?"

"Of course, who else?" The business manager sounded a bit peeved. "They need a nanny, and want a guy. But he wants you to go through an agency. I put in a good word."

A couple of phone calls later, and after I chatted with the agency, I had an interview. An interview that I very nearly wore a pair of stained pants to.

Mr. Black's butler met me at the door and led me into a wood-paneled office. A man who introduced himself as Mr. Black's house manager shook my hand and took a seat across the desk from me.

"So, Jeremy, are you gay?"

I gulped some of the Evian he'd given me (in a bottle, not a glass, which was interesting). I looked past him to the framed posters of Mr. Black's movies lining the walls, and I wondered if this was a trick question. As far as I could see, there wasn't a good reply. *Here goes nothing*, I thought. "No sir," I said.

"So you're straight?"

"Yes."

"Well, don't women you date find it strange?"

"Find what strange?"

"Oh, you know. A good-looking man, in pretty good shape, choosing to work as a nanny."

Clearly he didn't know the modern term for a male nanny, but I knew better than to correct him.

"Well, I haven't had any problems so far," I said, hoping man to man we could lighten the mood a little. In truth, I always thought of being a manny as similar to being a camp counselor, with fewer kids and a nicer car. What did women have to complain about? He wrinkled his brow; it looked like a frown, so obviously I wasn't scoring as many points with him as I did at the bar. "I tell women I'm a manny, and I work for private families but am not allowed to talk about it. Often women seem to really like the idea."

"Hmm," he said. "That seems reasonable. And what about your employers on that front, have you never had trouble with them?"

"I'm sorry? On what front?"

"You know, with the *wives*." He gave me a meaningful look.

"Oh, you mean about giving their daughters baths and things like that? My last job was with boys, but I did some babysitting before where girls were involved, and of course it was okay. I think it seems like it will be weirder than it is. I believe in addressing discomforts like that straight on, so we can move past them."

The house manager scrutinized my face for a bit longer. *What is his deal?* I wondered. *What is he searching for?* Does he think I'm a perv or something?

We talked for a half an hour more about my experience with troubled kids and about my flexibility (yes, I have a passport and, yes, I'm willing and eager to travel). I thought we were getting somewhere, and he seemed to like me. Then he said, "I'll arrange for a meeting with you and Mr. Black. I would certainly never suggest that you lie, but if he assumes you're gay, that's not necessarily a bad thing." Then he showed me the door.

TRACY

I wasn't at all sure I was ready for this interview. I was still getting used to the idea of not working for my old family. Over the years that I've been a nanny, I've heard all sorts of stories about horrible endings, but I'd never experienced anything like that. I'd left my most recent family on the best of terms; they just didn't need me anymore because the kids were older. I knew we'd keep in touch but it wasn't the same as being part of their lives every day. They threw me a beautiful party on my last evening with them, and gave me a fabric bag that looked just like the one in *Mary Poppins*. Inside was a tape measure, and, in keeping with the theme of *Mary*

Poppins, when you pulled it out, it was embroidered with "Tracy White . . . Practically Perfect in Every Way." I cried for a full three minutes after I opened it. I think they were surprised—they'd never seen me cry before, and probably didn't expect that their proper British nanny even could.

It's no secret that I was too invested in my work. The cardinal rule for nannies is "Don't ever forget this is not *your* family." Yet I have long believed that anything worth doing is worth doing 100 percent. I'm also convinced that it's the fact that I care so very much that makes me so good at my job. Tell Carson on *Downton Abbey* that the Granthams are not his family—he'd haughtily raise an eyebrow at you: "Beg your pardon," he'd say, "but what do you know about it?" The problem is, I live in an era when it's impossible to stay with one family for an entire career. Children get older. They stop needing you. But that doesn't mean it doesn't take some time to adjust.

All that said, this would be a good job. And they needed someone right away.

The parents were both directors, but not so recognizable that paparazzi was a problem. We met at a Starbucks, and no camera phones stealthily snapped pictures of them. No bodyguards stood nearby. Even better, they brought the baby with them. Colin was adorable, cherubic with blue eyes. I've never for a moment stopped loving babies—their soft skin and the way they marvel at such everyday things as their feet, a song, or a silly face. It would be lovely to take care of a baby again.

"Your reputation precedes you," said the dad, Mitch. "Seamus and Molly were sorry to see you go."

I smiled, but resisted saying much in return. It could be a trap—they could be trying to get me to open up about my previous employers, which led to the second rule of any good nanny: Never talk about your prior family.

"Our one concern," said the mum, Cathy, "isn't even about you, but about us, and how you'll manage with our lifestyle." She looked apologetic. "As Julie probably told you, travel is a large part of the job. Just in the next nine months, we're scheduled to be in Russia, Australia, Hong Kong, Belize, and Prague. I can't even think of where else at the moment . . . It's important to us not to leave Colin behind. He changes so quickly—we don't want to miss a thing."

I nodded my understanding. "Yes, I understand about the travel."

"And the schedule is pretty changeable," she added. "Much as I would love to lay out the next few months, things change with filming locations. I'm sure you can understand."

"It's fine," I said. "I love to travel. That's why I was keen to come to America in the first place. And don't worry," I added. "I don't even have a cat, to tell you the truth!" I laughed nervously then, because it somehow sounded sad when I said it out loud. But it wasn't . . . not really.

The mum and dad looked at each other, and I could see their relief.

"We'll be calling Julie this afternoon," Mitch said, and shook my hand.

We all stood up to leave. "Oh, and Tracy," Mitch called, before I walked out the door. "You might want to pack a bag. We're on a flight first thing tomorrow morning."

LAURA

I'm done with the über rich and famous. *Done.* I parked in a four-car carport—nice, but nothing shockingly extravagant. The mom met me at the door herself, not some butler or house manager. And she looked cool, understated—much more Jennifer Garner than Pamela Anderson.

I followed her through the house to the living room, which was elegant, but in a livable Pottery Barn way. The kids' artwork was pinned up on the walls, and I had to step over a Barbie Corvette to get to the couch. I knew a five-year-old girl and seven-year-old boy lived here, and it showed. It was real.

I had good reason to want real. I was from Oregon, which may as well have been another planet. Oregon did not have many rich people—aside from Nike folks, I guess. And if you were rich in Oregon you tried to hide it. You still rode your bike to work and grew your own kale. And you probably even played in a folk band and volunteered with the homeless on the weekends.

Don't get me wrong; I love Los Angeles. I love the sunshine, and that people wear something other than fleece.

People here value art, they value aesthetics. And they have lots and lots of money—all good things for a gal like me who's trying to put herself through school.

But there was another reason I wanted real. My last job had nearly given me a nervous breakdown. The family traveled constantly, which I knew going in, but with my school schedule, I'd told them I couldn't travel more than a week at a time. They'd agreed to it! Well, they must have had selective amnesia, because on a trip to London I was given my schedule for the next week, and it did not have us back in Los Angeles, as I'd been told we would be. Nope. We'd be in Budapest, which, if you really stop to think about it, has absolutely zero in common with LA.

When I asked what was going on, my bosses just said, "Oh, well, we need to stay. If you absolutely need to go home, then you'll need to buy a flight with your own money."

Well, I did absolutely need to go home. But a last-minute ticket from London to Los Angeles costs about $3,000. I felt stuck. And pissed. The mom was super skinny and weird about food, too, which was almost as bad as trapping me abroad. There wasn't anything to eat in the house we rented except chia seeds and agave, and no stores nearby. I had to walk two miles to the market to get bread and peanut butter. I mean, I didn't expect gourmet meals all the time, or even a lot of food on hand. But access to some food would have been nice.

I forked over my own money to fly home, and then I quit. The agency got me reimbursed later, but even so!

This job, in contrast, wouldn't pay as well, but I was okay with that. I'd happily trade cash for a little moral grounding. And I wanted a mom I liked—I would be spending a lot of my time with her, I knew. I wasn't looking for a friend, exactly, but if you work with someone day in and day out, shouldn't you be able to have a nice, pleasant conversation with her?

This mom's name was Lillian. We chatted on the couch for an hour, and she seemed so grounded. Which I guess shouldn't have been a surprise—she was a stay-at-home mom, not an actress. She'd worked as a makeup artist or something years before, which is how she met her designer-husband, James. They were one of the Hollywood marriages that seemed . . . well, normal-ish. He was a big name, but more likely to be featured in *Town & Country* than *People*.

When James came home, I liked him, too. "Tell us, Laura," he said, "what are you looking for in a family you work for?"

"People I connect with," I answered honestly. "People who value my opinion."

"Well, what's your opinion?" he smiled.

"Sorry? Of what?"

"Of child rearing. How do you think children should be raised?"

"Oh!" I was caught off guard. No one had ever asked this in such an open-ended way. Usually, my employers just expected me to raise their children according to their philosophy. Or perhaps they'd ask my opinion about a certain brand of formula, but never about how I thought their children should be raised. Oh, what the hell, I thought. Might as well answer honestly. If they hate what I say, and hold it against me for saying it even though they asked, then they're not a good fit anyway.

"Well," I began, "I give a lot of credit to my mom in the way she raised me. She was warm and loving, but also pretty firm. If I left one day to go to a friend's house and hadn't made my bed, which was my daily chore, she'd call the friend's house and have me sent home to do so—then and only then could I go back. A lot of my friends thought she was too strict, but I can see that she was right. I needed to learn responsibility, and her firm boundaries helped me learn that."

"I love that," said James. "I was raised that way, too. I completely agree."

I breathed again, but not before stealing a glance at Lillian, who was nodding her approval, too.

This was it, I felt sure. They were great, and they saw who I was and liked it. This was where I would be for years. I'd see the kids through to high school graduation, part of the family, but just professionally removed enough. Yes, I'd chosen some bad families in the past, but I'd learned. Now I would choose respect and normalcy over a huge paycheck, and still my payday would be pretty great.

I'd finally figured out how to do this nanny thing right. *Go Laura!*

CHAPTER TWO

· ·

The Charges

On RIE, Orgasmic Childbirth,
and Winston Churchill's Boyhood

The relationship between a nanny and her charges can often be beautiful, meaningful, and long lasting. The nanny becomes a lifeline between the traveling, active Hollywood parents and their often confused children. This creates deep and often complex bonds between the children and their nanny.

Once there was a lovely woman who gave her whole heart and soul to her work as a nanny. She spent her life taking care of others, and raised a dozen children who were not her own. She bandaged their knees, mended their fraying blankies, made sure they minded their manners, and helped them become thoughtful grown-ups. Unfortunately, she neglected to care for herself—a common occurrence for nannies—and she grew ill. There came a point when she decided against seeking further medical care, and as she rested through her final days, her ducklings came back to her to say good-bye. Many were grown, with families of their own, and some flew in from far away. So important was her role in their life that they needed to thank her, to tell her what an impact she'd had.

And then there's the story of one of our most esteemed countrymen, Winston Churchill, and his nanny. According to a Churchill biography, he and his nanny, Elizabeth Ann Everest, were uncommonly close. Churchill's mother was a remote, distant parent, and Mrs. Everest gave him unconditional love and caring. Churchill never forgot. When he had outgrown needing a nanny and Mrs. Everest was dismissed, he accused his mother of being heartless for letting her go without providing for her future well-being. He himself helped support her. He was beside her when she died, and organized and paid for the funeral himself, though he was only twenty.

Children have a way of touching a nanny in an indelible way as well. One five-year-old, let's call her Ellie, recently moved her nanny, Isabelle, in just such a way: Isabelle's boyfriend had broken it off with her, and the little girl heard her parents talking about how sad her nanny was. She drew Isabelle a card that showed a heart broken in half, and then mended together. "I'm sorry Greg broke your heart," the little girl said. "But look here—I fixed it." In a very real way, she *had* fixed it.

Whether you're raising a child in New Zealand, India, or Milwaukee, parenting challenges remain similar. But Hollywood has its own peculiarities (and not just ones related to wealth). Remember, first of all, these children were not born on the planet we were, they were born on Planet Hollywood. Unlike their parents, who in most cases grew up in modest households, these children came into a world where Kraft macaroni and cheese, leftovers, and hand-me-downs are unknown phenomena. When they ask a friend to come over and watch a movie, they are not talking about renting a DVD and eating some popcorn—they are talking about a private viewing of a new movie in a state-of-the-art screening room, where anything they want to eat will be prepared for them and delivered by the personal chef. Or, they can just help themselves to the screening room's candy store and ice-cream-sundae bar.

Once a nanny brought her Hollywood charge with her for a visit to Julie's Venice bungalow, and the child's eyes opened wide, as if he were on an African safari. "Wow! Her house is so small!" He tugged on his nanny's hand and said, "Why do people live in such small houses?"

Many a nanny has tried to instill her charges with a down-to-earth sensibility. Stella has often said to privileged children, "The people in your home provide a service. That doesn't mean they're your servants!" In reality, this message is as much for the parents as it is for the children, and Stella doesn't shy away from making this point to the entire family. The children aren't treating the staff poorly just because— they're treating the staff poorly because they've seen their parents do it. One manny we know suggested to the parents that he take their son on a commercial flight so he would have some familiarity with its customs. "Why?" asked the parents. "He'll always be able to fly private." Indeed, Stella was once in the company of a child who asked her, "Are we really taking a *public* plane?"

On another occasion Stella was tucking a charge into bed. They happened to be on this most fabulous yacht. (Imagine a Disney cruise, where everything conceivably desired is at your disposal.) It was Stella's habit, after she tucked him in, to go out to the deck and have a cup of tea. "No, Stella," he whined one night. "I'll miss you too much when I'm sleeping."

"Ah," Stella said. "Don't you worry, love. I'm going to be right outside, and besides—I need my cup of tea."

"No, I don't want you to leave," he insisted. "I want you to stay with me. Don't go—you can't go! Just call Hans!" the little boy said, Hans being the deckhand. He leapt out of bed and reached for the telephone. "He'll bring it to the room for you!" To Stella it was so endearing—he wanted her with him, and could kill two birds with one stone by getting her cup of tea delivered. In this little one's world, there was nothing that was out of his immediate reach, so there should be nothing that was out of his nanny's. One of the reasons Stella loved him (and loves him still) is because he wanted to bring her along for the luxurious ride.

But this sense of entitlement can backfire, and backfire big. Just take a quick Google search under "messed-up celebrity kids" and see how much comes up.

One nanny and butler wrapped a boatload of toys for a family's eight-year-old daughter's birthday. When the birthday came, the girl opened the gifts dismissively. After opening one of the less expensive gifts that didn't meet her liking, she said, "I hate my life. This birthday sucks."

The parents were devastated. The father turned to the nanny like a little kid himself, and asked, "How did this happen?" Then fury set in, and he shouted at his daughter: "Get out of my sight! You appreciate nothing!"

The nanny wanted to say it wasn't the girl's fault at all. Think about it: parents set the bar of expectations so high that nothing is exciting to the children.

Why would it be exciting for a boy to get a skateboard, when last year his parents built him a custom skate *park*? Parents buy more and more to alleviate their guilt—their guilt at being absent, and their guilt for not knowing their children's shoe sizes or friends' names. When they're on the set, mums feel guilty for not being with their kids. When mums are at home, they feel guilty for not being at work (they don't have a long lifespan in Hollywood!). And they feel guilty for not really relating to their kids. It becomes a no-win situation for them (one that, incidentally, Hollywood dads don't seem to share).

But it's more than guilt. Parenting rich kids is challenging, even if mum and dad are around a lot. Malcolm Gladwell even tackled this phenomenon in his book *David and Goliath*. He interviewed an extremely successful Hollywood producer who had grown up in a tough neighborhood, and under very difficult financial circumstances. His upbringing taught him the value of working hard, and led in no small way to his success. But how to teach that lesson to his own children, who clearly see their father's wealth and benefit from it?

"My own instinct is that it's much harder than anybody believes to bring up kids in a wealthy environment," the producer told Gladwell. "People are ruined by challenged economic lives. But they're ruined by wealth as well because they lose their ambition and they lose their pride and they lose their sense of self-worth. It's difficult at both ends of the spectrum. There's some place in the middle which probably works best of all."

Then, of course, Gladwell gets all *Gladwellian* about it and points to a U-curve that shows how challenging parenting is for low-income families, and how challenging it is for ridiculously high-income families, with the best bits coming for those in the middle.

"The man from Hollywood had too much money," Gladwell writes. "That was his problem as a parent. He was well past the point where money made things better, and well past the point where money stopped mattering all that much. He was at the point where money starts to make the job of raising normal and well-adjusted children more difficult."

If you've had a child any time in the last twenty years, you've heard of attachment parenting. This philosophy suggests parents wear their children in slings, co-sleep (sleep with them in one bed), and give them constant reassurance that mum and dad are always there to meet their needs. Attachment parenting, it's argued, gives children a strong sense of security and well-being. As the website of attachment parenting guru Dr. Sears claims, "When going from oneness to separateness (a process called 'individuation'), the securely attached toddler establishes a balance between his desire to explore and encounter new situations and his continued need for the safety and contentment provided by mother." Sounds good, but what if the adult offering the attachment parenting is the *nanny*? What if the *nanny* must sleep with the children each night, so that they feel secure and attached? We know of plenty of nannies who have had to share a bed with their charges. Another nanny had to sleep on a blow-up bed in the kids' room once they went to sleep—at 7:30! She wasn't permitted to read or watch TV, even with headphones, because she might wake the children. A 7:30 bedtime was not an easy adjustment for a nanny who was a night owl. And then what happens when she leaves? Because, you see, there's been a glitch: the children are attached all right—to *the nanny*, not the parents!

DESIGNER KIDS

Here's a little list of some of the more expensive items owned and enjoyed by the Hollywood munchkins.

1. $300 toddler dresses
2. $1,300 designer coats
3. Cashmere sweaters and blankets in all colors
4. $35 socks
5. $1,000 baby blankets
6. $100,000 themed birthday parties
7. $20,000 pieces of artwork for the nursery
8. $1 million nurseries
9. Backstage VIP passes to Katy Perry, Britney Spears, all things X Games, and The Wiggles (these can be worth tens of thousands of dollars)
10. $360,000 Maybach (a luxury German car) for a child's sixteenth birthday
11. Crystal-studded baby bathtubs (who even *knows* how much this costs?)
12. A custom-made bulletproof Mercedes SUV used exclusively for driving the children around

Then there's RIE (Resources for Infant Educarers), another parenting craze that suggests respect for a baby above all else. Under the RIE way, or at least the Hollywood RIE way, sippy cups, bouncy chairs, and things like Baby Björns are forbidden. Imagine being a nanny and bouncing around between RIE and attachment, attachment and RIE! So you see, we're looking at one fad that's too much, and one that's too little. A nanny must clear her head or she won't know whether to pick up the baby when he cries or to talk respectfully to him through his discomfort.

One of our favorite fads is the "child-led" parenting program, wherein a child's whims and creativity must be met at every level, and the child dictates the content and flow of the day. One nanny was appalled—but had to keep it to herself—when the twins she looked after were permitted to open the refrigerator, take out anything they wanted, and make a concoction in the middle of the kitchen floor. One particular concoction involved artisanal cheese, ketchup, a slice of lemon meringue pie, and a great deal of hummus. "It's artwork!" declared the mum (no, we are not kidding), and the household staff was forbidden to remove it for a week, even though it grew mold and attracted ants. What kind of message would removing it send to the twins about their brilliant creation?

And finally, many readers may have heard that Scientology has, um, *unconventional* practices for raising children. A nanny we know quit a job rather than continuing to feed the baby his, um, *unique* formula. And while there's much she can't and won't say, she did say this: If you really want to know what goes on with Scientology, read the *National Enquirer*. What you read there is *all* true. (Now, if she goes missing, we'll know who's taken her!)

While parenting fads are everywhere, they seem to be amplified and taken to an extreme in Hollywood. Don't forget that sometimes the reasons these philosophies become fads in the first place is because Hollywood celebrities have glamorized them.

HOLLYWOOD PARENTING FADS

RIE: Respect the baby above all else.

Attachment Parenting: Wear your baby—don't let them feel insecure for a split second.

Child-led Parenting: Pretty self-explanatory. The three-year-old runs the show!

Family Bed: The parents allow the children to sleep with them for as long as they want. Think mum, dad, twelve-year-old Johnny, eight-year-old Sarah, five-month-old baby, and the dog!

Indigo Children: A belief that children who come into the world acting like royalty are the beginning of a new consciousness, a new era of human beings.

Extreme Breastfeeding: A philosophy that holds that you should breastfeed your children until they want to stop—which could be well into their elementary school years.

Orgasmic Childbirth: This belief asks, "Why *shouldn't* you have an orgasm while you're having a baby?"

Bird-Style Feeding: Alicia Silverstone was a great fan of this strategy, wherein the mum chews up her child's food first, then feeds it to the child, mouth to mouth.

Placenta Encapsulation: The placenta is made into vitamin pills, and the mum takes them after she's had the child.

Elimination Communication: The practice of watching your infant's cues for when he needs to use the potty, and then holding him over the toilet. As Mayim Bialik has reportedly said, "Babies are born potty trained."

The relationship between the nanny and her charge is also amplified in Hollywood because of the sheer amount of time they spend together. In non-Hollywood families, the children are with the nanny for perhaps nine hours a day, five days a week. But in Hollywood, the parents work odd hours. If they're not working, they're likely to be anywhere but home wiping noses and refilling sippy cups. Nannies can be the earth, moon, and stars to these children. Soon they'll be attending the child's parent-teacher conferences, scheduling and taking them to doctor and therapist appointments, and organizing the children's social calendars. We always warn nannies not to get too close. We remind them that these children—and their lifestyles—are not the nannies'. They are borrowed.

It can be hard, undoubtedly. Nanny Lizzie grew very attached to a little boy she was with 24-7, four days a week. When the little boy took his first steps, Nanny Lizzie filmed it on her iPhone, and excitedly sent it off to the boy's mum. The mum's response: "Per our agreement, please only e-mail me, if necessary, at the end of your shift."

Another nanny, Amelia, told a rather heart-wrenching story of how she came into a family where the two little boys were completely unruly. Their parents were divorced and they lived with their mum, who was never around. After some time under their nanny's care, the boys started to pull themselves together. The staff, their friends, and their teachers all remarked on what a positive change they'd seen. But it was too intense. She was mother, father, *and* nanny to these boys. It was too much involvement, and she knew it. So she wanted out, and called her nanny agent.

Forty-five minutes later, the business manager called and fired her. To this day, the only way she can grasp the uncanny timing is that the phone was tapped, and the mum wanted to fire her before she could quit. Shocking, yes, but not actually the point of our story. The point was that Amelia had to leave the house—*right then*! She was only given a few minutes to say good-bye to the boys to whom she'd meant so much. And she was told she had to delete every picture of them from her phone.

"Your mom needs to make some changes," Amelia told the boys when she sat them down, "and I'm not going to be able to stay. But you are wonderful boys, and you are going to love whoever takes care of you next, and they are going to love you." They looked at her, crestfallen and confused.

Amelia held it together in the room with the boys, but she was furious. She called the mum's personal assistant and said, "Tell Fancy Pants she needs to come home now. If she's making me break their hearts, she has to at least be here for them!"

Then she walked out of the house forever.

If you're feeling like you want to slap this mother upside the head, please remember, this is *Hollywood*. Julie wanted to slap the nanny upside the head for getting way too invested in the job. There are some nannies that delight in being the person the child runs to when he's upset. Many parents who make quick switches like this have a good reason for doing so. Celebrity families are stalked by paparazzi, and there are many people out there who feed on them to make a living. It's a hard environment in which to trust anyone, let alone someone you have just fired, and who has been so intimately connected with you. It's horribly sad, of course, but you can't always blame parents for making abrupt changes. In many cases, they are just trying to protect themselves and their children, and who can fault them for that?

Not Too Much

Not getting too attached is one of the hardest things for a nanny to do. After all, the fact that she cares so much is what makes her good at her job. But these children are not hers. They must be returned one day. To keep the relationship healthy, she must love them . . . but not too much. They must love her . . . but not too much.

One of the little boys Stella took care of is without a doubt one of the great loves of her life. When she left that job, she felt like she lost a limb. She thinks about him all the time, and still sees him and his family, even though she hasn't been his nanny in years.

How to have attachment but not? In many ways, it's a matter of *degree*. There are some nannies we know who delight in the fact that the parents can't cope when the nanny isn't around; or that the child runs to them, and not the parents, when he falls over; or that—horror of horrors—the child refers to the nanny as "mummy." This is obviously too much attachment.

We end this chapter with a cautionary tale. Haley was a wonderful nanny who enjoyed her job working for billionaires. When her charge turned one, Haley worked with him as he learned to walk. Well, as anyone knows who has ever been around a toddler for more than a half second, they fall quite a bit. And this little boy fell one day. He got a good bump and had a good weep, but it was no big deal to anyone ... but the mum. Now, it was quite clear that this mum had a lot of guilt about her role in her child's life. She was a studio executive who worked upwards of sixty-five hours a week. It all came pouring down on Haley, in the form of micromanaging. The mum made it clear that it was not acceptable for her toddler to fall.

"This is too much pressure," Haley told her boss. "He's going to fall over sometimes. He hasn't really even started walking yet." The mum was unwilling to change her position, so Haley gave notice, or depending on how you look on it, she was fired.

KIRSTEN

As you might have guessed, I got the job. I am now a nanny for A-listers. Every day I work on the beach in Malibu. I can see the gorgeous ocean and swim in the pool with the kids. And the kids! They are awesome! (Well, they were at first ... more on that later.) The boy, Derek, is ten, and adorable in that super self-conscious way that ten-year-old boys are. Ali is eight, and she's up for anything and is possibly the most easygoing kid I've ever met. During our first few weeks together, we hung out on the beach almost every day. I'm a pretty firm nanny, and it didn't take them long before they got that and they seemed to respect it. They knew that to get "Fun Kirsten" and not "Strict Kirsten," they needed to listen to me.

Then, a couple of days ago, the house manager, Sasha, pulled me aside and said, "You know, you don't have to stay here with the kids all the time." I looked at her blankly; I had no idea why I wouldn't *want* to stay on the glorious beach with the kids all the time. At least until they started school again. And I had specifically been told to keep the kids close to home as Ron had a new movie coming out and the press were everywhere. Was I doing something wrong?

"Derek asked the other day if we could use their Disneyland passes, for a day out," I replied.

"That's a perfect idea," Sasha said. "I'll arrange for security to accompany you; how about tomorrow?" She ducked into her office mumbling something about passes.

"Oh?" I prodded, thinking she meant they had a season pass or something. She came out with these VIP passes. *Of course.* I was glad I hadn't shown my naïveté. *Of course* the children of Tess Gallant and Ron Powell wouldn't just have season passes to Disneyland—they'd have access to whatever they wanted throughout the whole park.

"We're bringing two friends each," Derek announced later at dinner. *Yikes*, I thought. *Six kids . . . let's hope one of the other families sends a nanny, too.*

At eight o'clock the next morning, a limo was waiting to take us to Disneyland, complete with our security detail. The cook had arranged to stock the car with pastries, fruits, and yogurts so we wouldn't need breakfast before we left. When we got to Anaheim, the car drove around to a separate entrance to the park—one I'd never seen before. I'm not sure I could even describe where it was if I wanted to—it was so disorienting not to go in the standard direction of the masses.

I should probably explain that I've been to Disneyland a few times in my life, and I liked it just fine, but it's usually so crowded and hot (Why so few trees, Walt? Why?) that I've spent most of my time in the Happiest Place on Earth cursing humanity while pondering which insanely long line is going to give me the most value for time spent waiting.

Let's just say this experience was different. I did not see a line all day. Or rather, I saw them, I just didn't wait in them. We had a park chaperone, who flashed a pass to a park employee near the ride we wanted to go on next, and he or she escorted us by way of the exit to the front of the line. We must have gone on the Indiana Jones ride a dozen times—before lunch! For every show or parade we wanted to see, we needed only to arrive a moment before it began, show our passes, and somehow spots would be found. Ali wanted to go to Ariel's Grotto for lunch, a princess-themed restaurant I'd heard you had to make reservations at weeks in advance—plus it was in a whole other park, California Adventure, with its own entrance. I bit my lower lip and explained to her that while I would try, she should try not to be disappointed if we couldn't pull this one off. She smiled at me. God, that girl is gorgeous! There is a reason people like her parents mate with one another . . . but I digress.

I asked our chaperone how we might go about going to Ariel's Grotto for lunch. He asked me to wait a moment while he made a call. When he came back, he explained that our table at the Grotto was waiting for us.

This was not the Disneyland I knew. This was a Disneyland with no hassle, no crowds, no waiting or planning your route, no uncomfortable sunburn or tired legs. This was Awesome Disneyland. I was giddy, and the kids must have felt it. They were more playful than they'd ever been with me, daring me to eat an entire Mickey ears ice cream sandwich in three bites (I failed), chasing me around Tom Sawyer Island, tickling me at the Haunted Mansion and pretending like they hadn't. Then, late in the day, when we went on Pirates of the Caribbean, Ali held my hand and I heard Derek tell one of his friends I was the best nanny so far. When night fell, we bought those glowing necklaces and linked arms all the way back to the limo, security dragging behind, carrying all our purchases. Back at the compound—oops, I mean house—the other kids all dropped off, I tucked Ali and Derek into bed and then drove myself home, thinking how lucky I was to have the absolute best job in the world.

But something happened today . . . some sort of switch flipped with Derek. Tess and Ron were supposed to be home from a trip abroad, but had to delay their return for some reason or other. I was in the room while he was on the phone with them, and he didn't seem that upset. Just a lot of "yeah . . . that sounds good . . . I miss you, too." Ali was more clearly disappointed, I could tell. I asked her if she wanted to talk about it, and her eyes filled up with tears. "Yes!" she blurted, and ran into my arms.

"I know it must be hard," I soothed. "I know you must miss them. But they love you very much, and they'll be back soon." She sniffled and let me rub her back until she felt better. Then she asked if I'd play dress up with her, which I have to tell you is unlike any game of dress up I've ever played. It basically involves real Prada and Chanel. She put on high heels, which she's never allowed to wear out of the house, and begged me to do her hair and makeup, just like she sees people do for her mother all the time.

Derek kept mostly to himself, which I thought was fine—he needed to deal with his disappointment in his own way. I let him play his video games while Ali and I played dress up, but then told him he'd just get to play for another ten minutes.

"You can't tell me what to do," he announced. "You're not my mother." I was a bit shocked, because he'd never taken that tone with me.

"No, I'm not, but I *am* in charge."

"No," he said. "I am. I can get you fired."

He had my full attention. Who was this creature? Where was the boy who tickled me at Haunted Mansion?

"Oh?" I said. "And just how do you plan to do that?"

"Easy," he said. "I'll throw myself against this wall until I get a bruise, and then I'll tell my parents you did it."

"They wouldn't believe you," I countered, completely unsure whether that was true or not. *Be strong, Kirsten . . . he's testing you. Don't let him see he's freaking you out.*

"Why would they believe *you*?" he said. "They don't even know you."

I sat down at his level and looked him full-on in the eye. *Be firm. Be compassionate. Be consistent.*

"Here's the thing, Derek," I said softly. "I think you're upset because your parents aren't home when they said they'd be. I think you miss them. It makes you feel like they don't care. And so you're mad, and I'm here for you to take it out on. Maybe you think if you get rid of me, your parents will have to come home sooner. Or stay home longer. But that's not what would happen. They'd replace me in a minute, with someone else who does the same stuff I do, but who probably doesn't look as cool while doing it."

He was quiet, and so was I, for as long as I could stand it.

"So," I said, "I'm going to go get you some milk and fruit from the kitchen, and when I get back, the Xbox is going to be off."

I walked out before he could say another word. And when I returned, the Xbox was off. I'd won round one. But until today, I hadn't even known whom I was up against.

JEREMY

This job is a lot more intense than I thought it was going to be. One kid, that's it: a twelve-year-old boy named Chase. Two parents, one of whom (Mr. Black) travels 95 percent of the time. Mrs. Black is around a fair amount, and she's cool—I like her. She's always saying really nice things about me.

But the kid. That's the problem. If I get a degree in child psychology, I'm sure I'll understand what's going on with him in a different way. But right now, I don't have the expertise to know anything other than he's got issues. He's angry—a lot. And when he's angry, he's physical. On more than one occasion I've had to wrestle him to the floor and pin his arms behind his back to make sure he didn't hurt himself or anyone else. It's sort of like he is about to blow, and I just hold him until he calms down. I see why they needed a guy for this job.

The thing that kills me is that he's actually a great kid. He's hilarious, and can mimic everyone from the Bronx-born housekeeper to the chauffeur with the heavy Irish brogue. He's smart, and his memory must be close to photographic—he can recall verbatim magazine articles he's read. I swear, when I look at him after he's had one of his violent fits, he looks so . . . I don't know, freaked out. He's this really skinny kid with huge eyes, and when he gets scared like that, I just want to protect him from himself.

So here's what happened today. It was my day off and I was doing some yard work for my mom when my cell rang. It was Mrs. Black, and she was kind of hysterical. I couldn't make out much of what she said except "Can you please come?"

"Yes, I can come, but I'm having a hard time understanding you. What's going on?"

She took a breath and tried to tell me again. "Chase got into an argument in science class today and I guess he hit his lab partner. The teacher tried to get control and couldn't, and Chase ended up running down the hall and locking himself in a supply closet. No one can get him to come out. Can you please come to the school and talk to him? He'll only listen to you!"

"Where are you?" I asked, trying not to imply that I thought she should handle it herself, but wondering why she wasn't.

"I'm here at the school, of course!" she shot back. "I've been pleading outside the locked door for a half an hour. I'm scared—what if he hurts himself? And I can't reach Mr. Black, like always." Her voice was thick with bitterness.

"Isn't there an extra key? I mean, can't security get in there somehow and handle it?"

She sighed. "Yes, but then what? He's having an incident." She whispered the word "incident," like it was something new or secret, instead of being right there for all to see at the school. "I don't want him to hit someone else. It's bad enough he struck that kid in class. I don't want this getting any more out of hand than it already has."

"I'll leave right now," I said. Normally, it's against my policy to drop everything to go to the aid of my employer. There are boundaries, after all—I have a life. But this seemed like a suitable exception.

When I got to the school, I checked in at the principal's office, and they told me where I could find Mrs. Black. She was sitting on a chair in the hallway outside a closet door, her head in her hands.

"Thank God!" she said when she saw me. "Chase!" she shouted into the door. "Jeremy's here. I'm going to leave you two for now!"

She gave me a squeeze on my arm, and her high heels clicked down the marble hallway. I sat in her chair.

"Hey buddy," I said. "Sounds like you had a crappy day." I couldn't hear much, just scuffling of some sort on the other side of the door. "Listen, can you just let me know if you can hear me? I really don't want to talk to myself."

Silence for a minute, then, "Yeah, I can hear you."

"So what's in that closet that's so exciting?

Silence again, then, "I don't know, nothing."

"Dude," I said, "you lost your cool. It's not good, it's definitely not good, but it's not the end of the world. We'll figure it out."

Silence.

Then I said, "Man, come on and let me in. I'm here for you, okay? We'll figure this out—it's no biggie—don't sweat it."

And then the door clicked. I opened it carefully. Chase had moved back to a spot in the corner and was wedged between shelves of cleaning supplies. He was curled into a ball; it looked kind of silly since he was becoming a big kid. I've never seen someone look more like they wanted to hide, to disappear. I was worried. This kid needed help, and more help than I could give him. I resolved I would talk to his mom—urge her to switch his therapist, get Mr. Black involved, too, if it was the last thing I did. It was time to call in the big guns and get this kid straightened out.

But I didn't say any of that then. I just sat next to him for a while.

"Ready to go?" I asked him.

"Ready," he said, and he slipped his hand into mine.

TRACY

Hong Kong is not the ideal place to get sick, especially if you are only eighteen months old. Poor Colin.

We'd been having such a lovely time. He didn't seem to mind Hong Kong's humidity, and wanted to be outside all the time. Hong Kong has these escalators that take you up an entire hillside. It's like a long, vertical market, and Colin loved it. We went up and down, up and down. He couldn't get enough of all the colorful dragon puppets, lanterns, and dangling knickknacks for sale all over the place. It was stimulation overload, but he showed no sign of tiring of it.

In the evenings, Cathy and Mitch delighted in giving him bites of new foods—pot stickers and sticky buns and everything else a baby could handle that tasted like China. I've never had a child be so *enthusiastic* about everything. I swear, he rarely cried. If he was tired, he'd rub his eyes or his ears, but he wouldn't fuss. If he was hungry, he'd grunt "eat!" or make the sign for it, as I'd been teaching him baby sign language. Each evening, Cathy and I would compare notes about the many ways he'd been delightful that day, and how exceptional this child was.

So that's why I knew right away that something was wrong when he started acting fussy. At first I thought, *Finally he's showing signs of being a normal baby!* But just in case, I took his temperature: 101 degrees Fahrenheit—not good for a baby. Then when I tried to give him some of the oatmeal he usually adored, he wouldn't touch it. Cathy didn't want to overreact, so I gave him a little infant Tylenol, lots of fluid, and we took it easy for the day. When he woke up the next morning, still fussy, I took a close look all over his little body, and saw two small sores breaking out on his buttocks.

"Ah," I said to Cathy. "I think he has hand, foot, and mouth disease."

Her eyes grew large with alarm. "You mean the cow thing?"

"No, no," I reassured her. "It's not that dire—it's just a virus, common in children. But it's uncomfortable. We should take him to the doctor."

Cathy and Mitch knew of an American-style health-care center, and felt more comfortable taking him there. Cathy called the doctor, and when she hung up the phone she called me in.

"The doctor said he's teething," she explained. "He said the sores are nothing to worry about—probably just chafing from the humidity."

"He's wrong," I said. I might not be a doctor, but I've taken care of children for a long time, and I know hand, foot, and mouth disease when I see it.

Cathy looked at me for a moment, trying to decide. Then she nodded her head. "Let's take him in." We loaded a still very fussy Colin into a taxi and made our way. I waited in the lobby while she took him in to see the doctor. After a while Cathy came out and beckoned to me.

"Tracy?" the doctor said, extending his hand for me to shake. He seemed very nice, but very young. I wondered what his qualifications were for this post. "I just wanted to thank you. You were right. I examined the sores, and Colin does have hand, foot, and mouth."

Cathy patted my shoulder, smiling. I felt like a Crufts show dog or something, but know she didn't mean it that way. In fact, quite the opposite—she just wanted to make sure I got credit where it was due.

I can't say that the week that followed was fun. Colin was extremely uncomfortable as the sores broke out all over his little mouth, and all over his body. It was a full-time task just to make sure he got the fluids he needed. But I made him as comfortable as I could, and took great pride that we were doing everything possible. And Cathy and Mitch, though always kind to me, treated me differently after that. I was now their parenting partner. They trusted me completely. Even more important to me, so did Colin.

LAURA

I know this sounds bad, but how is it that I am a single twenty-two-year-old and I know more about parenting than Lillian, who has been a mother for almost seven years now and reads every book about childcare that she can get her hands on? She must not really read them.

I'm sorry, that's unkind, I know. I'm just frustrated. I really like Lillian. I like her so much, in fact, that if we were the same age and I didn't work for her, we'd be good friends. She's light and funny and super easy to talk to. And she loves her kids to pieces. She doesn't work, so she's home with us a lot. Most of the time, actually. James is great, too, but he works all the time. In fact, I've got the sense that I'm there to be Lillian's friend as much as I'm there for the kids. If I tell her I'm taking them to the park or to the grocery store, she's always eager to join us.

Now for the kids. They're sweet . . . and out of control. But I'm working on it. Kylie is six, and Caleb is four. When I started a few weeks ago, they were total slobs. No sooner was the house picked up than it was a disaster again. They'd drop their jackets in the front hallway, leave their dishes wherever they were when they finished eating, and didn't have a single responsibility. They ate junk food because it was all they liked. They talked back to their mom, and to me.

None of this was cool. I felt like Nanny McPhee or something, rounding them up and letting them know there was a new sheriff in town and we were going to be doing things differently. We came up with a list of rules that we posted on the refrigerator. I started a marble jar: if they listened to me, I put a marble in the jar; if they talked back, they lost one. I promised we'd do something special when the jar was filled up. I put together a chore chart, so they would each know what they were responsible for each and every day, and I included things like making their beds, putting away their clothes, and setting the table. We went outside for fresh air and exercise every day, and I told them that if they didn't eat what I made them, they didn't eat.

At first I was worried that Lillian would think I was taking it too far, that I was being too strict with the kids and stepping on her turf. But she was enthusiastic about all the changes. She kept asking me questions about discipline strategies, about what to do when they whined, about how to handle it when they talked back. It didn't take me long to realize that I was nanny, coach, friend, and, in a way, Lillian's husband. I was up for the challenge. I loved it—I loved all the trust and responsibility she gave me.

Then two things happened last week that gave me pause. The first was when we were all at the park. Caleb was running around like a madman, as usual, and he fell and scraped his knee pretty badly. Lillian and I were sitting on a bench in the shade, and Caleb hobbled over to us, crying . . . and tried to climb on my lap for comfort. *Shit*, I thought. *Not good, not good.* A kid coming to his nanny when his mom is right there is exactly the kind of thing that could get you fired. I cast a sidewise look at Lillian, who was sitting still—her face a stony mask.

"Caleb," I whispered into his ear, "look, your mommy's right there—let's have her kiss it and I'll go look for a Band-Aid." I held my breath as I transferred him from my lap to hers. Would he protest? Would she hold it against me if he did? Was it already too late?

I went to the car to get the first-aid kit, and when I came back Lillian was tickling Caleb and they were both laughing. But when she saw me, her face was stone again. *Shit*.

KRAMER VS. KRAMER

You know that old stereotype about how mum is always the bad guy, making the kids eat and get dressed and clean their room while dad gets to play with them? Well, when a nanny's in the picture, the mums often feel freed from the role of bad guy—but, unfortunately, this is to the detriment of the children's discipline and consistency!

Nanny Chantelle complained to us one day that she worked really hard to set boundaries with her charges, but the mum undermined her at every turn. One particular night, she fed the kids dinner and told them they had to finish if they wanted a Popsicle. The little girl, Kelly, moved her spaghetti around on her plate, but didn't eat a bite.

"Time's almost up, guys," Chantelle said. "In five minutes, we're going upstairs to have a bath, so you need to finish eating." The little boy finished quickly, and Chantelle gave him a Popsicle. Kelly had a total fit.

"I WANT ONE, TOO!" Her little fists clenched and her face got red.

"Sorry, Kelly—time's up, and you didn't eat your dinner. Let's go on up to the bath."

"NO!! I WANT MY POPSICLE!"

"No," Chantelle said. "You knew the rule. Now I am going to take your brother up. When you've calmed down, you can come upstairs and join us in the bath."

Chantelle listened to her hysterics from upstairs, but wasn't fazed. She just focused on scrubbing the little boy in the bath, figuring Kelly would calm down and get with the program. A few minutes later, Kelly came upstairs looking triumphant. She was holding a Popsicle.

"Mom said I could have one," she said. *Ha ha!* she might as well have added.

Great, Chantelle thought. *Way to undermine your nanny.*

When mum came upstairs herself a few minutes later, she was all smiles and light.

"She really wanted that Popsicle!" she said, laughing. But the subtext was clear: *Remember who really calls the shots around here.*

CHAPTER THREE

· ·

The Sex

And Throw in Some Sensibility, Too

Jane Austen wrote the first draft of *Elinor and Marianne* (later retitled *Sense and Sensibility*) when she was in her early twenties. The plot of her story revolves around the contrast between Elinor's sense and Marianne's emotionalism, both elements Hollywood also struggles to balance. On the surface, Marianne loves hard and without caution . . . similar to how people plow through their relationship with Hollywood. Meanwhile, Elinor masks her emotions to a point that she almost chokes. She is filled to her throat with unshed tears, and throughout our favorite movie version (oh Emma Thompson, you are divine!), continually places a palm on her stomach to quiet her unresolved distress.

Ah, the complexities of sexuality, be it explored or repressed. Sex is just such a *rich* topic (no pun intended). Jobs are won and lost because of sex. An entire genre of books and movies exists because of sex. Heroes are brought down because of sex (oh Tiger; oh Arnold). Villains are made because of sex (see Angelina Jolie circa 2005). Tabloids are built upon the foundation of sex. Entire governments—no, entire kingdoms—have fallen because of sex. And Hollywood is one of the most sexualized cultures in the world. Though there might be a hint of sexuality on Fleet Street and Main Street (think holiday parties), in Hollywood, there's an entire boulevard dedicated to it: Sunset Boulevard. And inside most celebrity homes, it's not uncommon to find the air thick with the stench of sex. You catch whiffs of distrust, assumption, and fear laced through conversations—all of which the unfortunate nanny is privy to. Marriages once powered by sex are bruised and battered by sleepless nights, guilt, time apart, and an industry that shows no mercy for aging. Sex is power, sex is currency, sex is oxygen here.

So what happens when nanny, who has a front row seat to the sexual frustrations of mum and dad, finds herself between them, or in the unlucky position of playing referee? When there are problems in a marriage, the parents look for a place where they can have some pseudo closeness—like finding a common enemy—and for many, the nanny becomes a convenient target. Any slight mistake the nanny makes allows the parents to forget their current relationship trials and close rank. After one nanny was fired, the dad called her apologetically, explaining how over his wife's neurosis he was; he said nanny was just the most recent casualty. However, when her termination letter arrived, he had signed his name, aligning himself with all the mum's accusations. This is called Nanny Triangulation, and the nanny is caught in the middle of something she definitely, definitely wants no part of.

Celebrities' defenses are dropped at home. The well-crafted false personas are left in the dressing room or at the set, and a big deep breath reminds them that, regardless of stature, wealth, or celebrity, they are mere humans after all. Now imagine Jude Law. He's wearing boxers and his favorite worn-out basketball T-shirt, and being his vulnerable, pizza-eating, pet-loving, soap opera–watching self. Now imagine how adorable the family's nanny wants to appear to him. She works hard to anticipate his desire for a sandwich, orders his special sparkling water. When he asks her to list her favorite movies, she lists four of his movies in her top five. To him, she must seem like an angel, the perfect mother to his children, as she gracefully, and with a large dollop of experience, not a spoonful of sugar, tends to the children's moment-by-moment needs. Ethan Hawke and Mick Jagger are two more dads who have had difficulty maintaining, um, professional *distance* from their nannies. Eloise Parker said it well in the *NY Daily News*: "Watching Ethan Hawke settle down with his kids' former nanny is bound to send a shiver down the spine of many women who rely on professional help" ("Ethan

Hawke Wedding Spotlights Men's Attraction to Nannies," July 15, 2008).

Do you wonder if the stereotype of the predatory male heartthrob is true? It isn't. Except when it is. Julie once received a frantic call from a nanny visiting Costa Rica, where she'd traveled with the dad and the kids on an adventure holiday. The dad, as it turned out, wanted to show her his testicle piercings, and wasn't thrilled with taking no for an answer. Another dad suggested that his nanny jump on the trampoline with the kids, and then turned the hose on her to get her T-shirt wet. She immediately climbed off the trampoline, only to be chased by the dad with his hose! (Down, girls—we're talking about the *water* hose.)

Sometimes the passes are more subtle, such as when a dad gave the nanny a key to his office, and told her to let him know if she wanted to make some extra money filing papers for him. Filing papers, you see, is a euphemism for . . . well, in England we call it having sex. This poor nanny didn't realize that, and said, "Sure, thanks. I'm always looking for ways to make extra cash." When, excited at the possibility of making extra income, she told her boyfriend about it, he went ballistic. "Any task that you need your own key for is not what it seems!" he warned. She listened, and never took the dad up on the offer.

Later, the dad's passes became more overt. "Sometimes workplace relationships really work," he said out of the blue one day. "You know, I have several colleagues who have married their nannies." Now that this nanny was no longer so naïve, she saw this comment for what it was. "That's nice," she said. And followed it immediately with, "I met my boyfriend at my last job. I'd love for you guys to meet him sometime."

Thirty-one-year-old Lucy learned early in her career how to put lecherous dads in their place. "I was driving myself, my boss, and his friend and coworker home from dinner since they were tipsy. The mom and kids were out of town. She wanted me to make sure her husband always had dinner, and that also meant joining him for dinner if he wanted me to. I don't know what the mother was thinking, as she knew her husband had a wandering eye. So . . . that night while driving the two men home, the father was sitting behind me. He started caressing my neck and shoulders. I was driving and his friend was in the passenger seat.

"I felt humiliated, wondering what his friend might have thought was going on. I told my boss to stop in the most kind, appropriate way, but he didn't get the hint and began to stroke and blow on my neck. A while later my boss asked me to pull over to the side of the road so he could go to the bathroom. When he got out of the car, I looked over at his friend and said, 'Should I pull away so he's in plain sight of the cars driving by?' His friend laughed and thought it was a good prank and I thought it was a good way to give him the hint to stop touching me. I knew he wouldn't fire me. So, I pulled away and drove about a hundred feet and stopped. My boss freaked out, zipped up, and ran back to the car. He wasn't too happy.

I told him quietly that paybacks aren't fun, and he knew what I meant."

Sally, a nanny from Ireland, was in St. Bart's with a family, minus the mum. Sally was playing in the ocean with the kids, and the dad watched her every move from a beach chair. When she walked up to grab towels for the kids, he said, "If you want to keep throwing them in the air, great. And if you want to go Amazonian and take your top off, it's cool with me." The nanny never wore a bikini to work again, but invested in some long-sleeved, burka-esque rash guard swimming ensembles. (Why on earth did she think it was okay to wear a bikini to work in the first place? *Really!*)

WORK ATTIRE FOR DUMMIES

OKAY	NOT OKAY
one piece	bikini
granny knickers	visible thong
button-down blouse	low V-neck T-shirt (especially when worn with a push-up bra!)
mum jeans	baggy boyfriend jeans
mum jeans	skinny-leg jeans
mum jeans	jeggings
mum jeans	low-rider jeans

OKAY	NOT OKAY
mum jeans	holey jeans (and we don't mean blessed by the pope)
shorts to the knee	Daisy Dukes (although we do love Jessica Simpson)
hidden body art	in-your-face (or on-your-face) body art
little stud earrings	earlobe spacers
Mary Janes or Vans	stripper stilettos or any shoe without a back

This information has been compiled over the past twenty years based on nannies getting vetoed by parents for at least one of the above.

Rumor has it that Jude Law blamed then-fiancé Sienna Miller for his uncontrollable need to shag the nanny of his children. OMG, Jude . . . seriously! Jude Law aside, why does Hollywood think it's okay to blame a tired, flustered, over-worked mother for her partner's alley cat behavior? (Okay, well, perhaps "overworked" is a stretch for the celebrity mum who usually has 24-hour care for her new baby, but she is technically a "mum" now, and that alone is heaps of mental stress for many!) But one assumes that if anyone can work that excuse, it's Jude.

Calls about pervy dads are never fun to get, but they're simple enough to handle. Nanny keeps her distance and Julie threatens the business manager with a sexual harassment suit if dad doesn't. It's pretty clear-cut. But before you call foul on the male species, you should know that when it comes to matters of sex, it's not just about dads behaving badly. Mums and nannies are no saints, either.

Mums are a tough sexual nut to crack, so let's break it into categories. There are the cougar mums who lust after their male nannies and don't really bother to hide it from anyone. Mike, a former manny, reported this of his experiences: "Of course the lonely Hollywood housewife, coked to the gills and angry at the absent husband who justifies his abandonment as maintaining her lifestyle, would often approach the strapping young lad of twenty-two for a little afternoon TLC. If you wanted a sport fuck in my manny days the male nanny was *the* accessory for a side tryst. After all, the pool boy or tennis instructor was so cliché."

There are the mums who take a lighthearted approach to the whole thing, such as the one who called her nanny "Stripper Nanny" because she had such a good body, or the mum who would say to her nanny—joking—"So, whose turn is it to sleep with my husband tonight? Do I have to, or will you take the job?" She was kidding, of course . . . or was she?

And then there are the mums who are the most dangerous to the nanny—the ones who are insecure. One mum we know of came up to her nanny, looked straight at her chest, and asked her if her breasts were real. The dad asked the nanny to stop wearing V-necks because they were upsetting his wife. Another couldn't bear for her nanny to wear Lululemon yoga pants to work, so concerned was she about the perkiness of the nanny's bottom. "I'm here to do a job, nothing more," this very direct nanny couldn't help but say to her boss one day. But direct as she was, what she really wanted to say was, "If you can't trust me to be in the presence of your husband, you've got much bigger problems than your nanny's yoga pants, my friend!"

Yes, these mums are insecure, but let's not forget where they're coming from. Many of them feel tired and often haggard, and resentful that the nanny gets to come in and be the perfect one, like Maria to the von Trapp kids—expertly dancing with the talented children, a guitar case slung casually over her shoulder and a smile on her cherry-red lips. Mum herself doesn't often get to play this role.

Remember, too, that Hollywood female celebrities are hounded by a bevy of younger competitors all desperate for her life. They chase after her husband, her boyfriend, her contacts, her career, and her friends. The wannabes copy her fashion sense, which is sometimes flattering, but also a bit creepy. The wannabes imitate her hairstyle, her hand gestures, and her adorable walk (think Meg Ryan and Julia Roberts). Then, when her tummy begins to loosen around her cultivated six-pack, she will be dumped by her fans, and probably her husband. Hollywood is a fickle and unforgiving lover.

In short, there's just so much more subtext with these mums than the normal mum, and the issue of sex is the hardest to manage with them. They may even confide in the nanny about marital problems, and then hate her for knowing all about their business when she and the husband make up.

X-RATED PLAYDATE

Ingrid, a Swedish nanny working for a family in Santa Monica, couldn't understand why she was even needed to watch the kids when the dad was home, or when he invited all of his male friends and their kids over for a playdate. Surely between all of them, they could handle the kids? Sometimes there would be as many as a half dozen dads sitting around the pool, wearing their Ray-Bans, chatting on their cell phones to their offices, watching their children play. It wasn't until the mum came home unexpectedly one Friday afternoon that she understood. "Um, Ingrid?" the mum began. "In the US, it's not customary to swim topless."

Which leads to the subject of the nannies themselves. They are not always innocent victims here! While most nannies have no sexual interest in their employer, some will feel intoxicated by proximity. Imagine this: Nanny spends the summer tending the children on the beach in Malibu—akin to the Hamptons on the East Coast. She will *not* dress like Mary Poppins. She's got a great body, let's not forget, and it's warm, so she will wear skimpy tank tops and bathing suits while she runs in and out of the ocean with the kids. She will get swept up in the parties and the gorgeous guests and forget that she is not really part of this world herself . . . until mum's friends notice and draw mum's attention to the threat lurking in the waves. Then nanny will be fired, and must wave good-bye to the family forever.

Or perhaps nanny is with the family somewhere on a yacht in the Riviera, and when her bosses offer her a glass of (excellent) wine when she is off duty, trying to make her feel like "part of the family," she will accept it. When the father's Dashing Best Friend, who is also aboard the yacht, asks her for her number, she will give it to him. She will later go out with him, mortifying the mum at the very idea of a double date with *the help*! On one of her dates with Dashing Best Friend she will forget herself after her third glass of champagne and will talk about work. Perhaps she'll spill information about something innocuous like the gift that she helped the dad pick up for the mum. Weeks later, Dashing Best Friend will play a round of golf with the dad and the indiscretion will slip out—again, innocently—something like, "So how did your wife like that Hermès scarf? Nanny told me she helped pick it out." Treacherous. First an Hermès scarf slip, and then what? The condoms that nanny found in the bathroom garbage? The fight the parents had the week before? Worse yet, if the mum finds out that the nanny was involved in picking out the scarf, look out! She'll get sacked that same afternoon.

NAUGHTY NANNIES

There is just no excuse for the indiscretions of the following three nannies:

Kim: Kim had a huge crush on her actor boss, and one rainy LA evening, when mum was at a screening, she slipped out of her clothes and into the steam room in hopes of sharing some one-on-one quiet time with dad. "Mr. S., I know you've been wanting me," she said in her heavy German accent as she dropped her towel. Kim wondered why she was fired! We wondered how mum found out, and how soon dad told her!

Mary: Mary, Mary, Mary, you don't date the parents, especially both of them at the same time, and especially not together.

Louise: Well, there is much we could share about Louise . . . deep breath. Louise thought it would be fun to serve little martini mixers out of the trunk of her celebrity family's Mercedes. It gets worse . . . she was serving the mixers to all her Malibu nanny friends outside the *elementary school* as they waited for the kids. Okay, this one isn't about sex, but pretty appalling nonetheless.

To these nannies we say, "Get it together! Boundaries! Judgment! Transparency!" If her employers offer a glass of wine, even if she's off duty, there is only ever one answer: no. Even one drop of alcohol in mum and dad's presence could be held against her later on—it's just not worth it. If Dashing Best Friend asks her out, she should say, "Thank you, I'm flattered. Let's revisit that topic when I'm no longer working for your friends." Clothing should be chosen to *cover up*, not to *reveal*. Once Julie had a nanny come in wearing a low-cut V-neck shirt that showed off her ample bosom quite well. "It's a Gap shirt, just like you told me to wear!" protested the nanny when Julie gave her a look. "Yes," Julie explained, "but you're gapping out of it."

Hollywood is the most sexualized culture a person could possibly work in. In corporate culture, attractive women are encouraged to emphasize their looks, but nothing could be further from the truth in the world of the Hollywood nanny. Even at the interview stage, Julie's clients will tell her, "Please don't send anyone too pretty." Even if mum's not insecure, a sexy nanny could indicate a potential complication, and that's a red flag you don't want to wave at an interview.

So what does all of this mean, really, for the nanny? Does it mean that she must be asexual, that she must never even think a sexual thought while she is in this occupation? Of course not. What she does on her own time is her business, although she should take care not to share too much about it with her employers. Plenty of nannies meet and marry the loves of their lives during the time they are employed as a Hollywood nanny. But it is not easy to start and build a relationship when your primary relationship is with your work, when the lives of your employers come first, and when you don't get to even spend the holidays with your own family. It's a challenge to explain to your new beau that you can't go on a date because you may or may not be in the country that night.

All Is Fair in Sex and Nannywood

Scandalized, are you? Goodness, we hope not. It's just sex, people! We thought you were made of tougher stuff!

But there is another category of trouble lurking: *l'affair*. Sometimes the nanny *is* the affair; sometimes she's asked to help cover it up. One mum requested that her nanny vacate the cottage she lived in on-site for an hour each Monday—which coincided neatly with the time the dad's best friend came. Such a cliché! And yet so, so true, and requiring so many changes of sheets for the nanny. And sometimes dad knows about the affair, and has his own that the mum knows about. And sometimes it's even all open and plays out in front of the children. In one family the nanny was shocked when she came in one morning and found the mum snuggling on the couch with her lover, while the children slept in sleeping bags on the floor around them. Where was dad? Staying over at his girlfriend's, of course. This brings up a whole new set of Sex Ed questions from the children that nanny must be prepared to hear, if not answer.

LOVE ACTUALLY

Dating while working in Nannywood is a routine that Stella knows firsthand. She was working two nanny jobs and quite exhausted when she received a voice mail one day. It went like this: "Hey, Stella, I called your number by mistake to order a pizza. I love your accent. You sound very interesting. If you're single, give me a call." She liked the sound of his voice, too, so she called him back. After talking for a bit, she decided he wasn't a mass murderer, and told him that maybe she'd give him a call back sometime, and she did, two weeks later. He said, "You took your time."

She had nanny friends who told her it would never work out, as she had just signed a contract to work as a 24-7 baby nurse for four months. You work too much, they said, and no man would put up with that at the beginning of the relationship. She'd have to choose. But she also knew the right man would understand, that he would wait. That wrong number is now her partner of fifteen years and the father of her child. There are happy endings, there are.

One of our favorite stories is of the nanny who was asked to spend one night a week at the family's fancy downtown apartment with them. "Please keep your door open," the parents requested, "so that you can hear the baby if he cries." The nanny complied, and was surprised when the parents kept their door open, too. That surprise turned into mortification when the parents began to have very animated sex. Nanny ducked under her covers and put the pillow over her ears. She thought perhaps they'd just forgotten themselves . . . until they repeated the whole routine the next week. And then the week after that. *How do you ask your bosses to please not have loud sex when they're essentially sharing a room with you?* she wondered. She never asked the question. She just bought earplugs.

Even if nanny does everything right, even if she's asexual and appropriate, and even if the dad's not a perv and the mum's not insecure, it can all go awry if she is in the wrong place at the wrong time. This happened with a nanny we know, who was accidentally witness to the wife belittling—emasculating is really the better word for it—her husband. The mum didn't realize anyone else was in the room until something in her husband's eye caused her to turn. Nanny had seen and heard everything. *This is it*, that seasoned nanny knew. *I'd better start packing.* And indeed, she was sacked the next week.

The long and the short of it is this: when it comes to the issue of sex, mayhem is always just around the corner. Just as a family looks for a reason not to hire a nanny, they also look for a reason not to keep her. If it seems like the nannies can't win, well, that's somewhat true. But they *can* walk the tightrope, do the dance, and try to stay out of the ring or the bedroom for as long as possible. And if we haven't mixed our metaphors enough to scandalize you, then you are made of tougher stuff after all.

KIRSTEN

Tess and Ron finally returned, and Derek settled down a little bit. But only a little bit, because they came back with a tension between them everyone could feel. And hear, for that matter. Something must have happened on their trip, because Tess and Ron were constantly yelling. And I do mean yelling. Or do I mean screaming? Ali just tunes it out—literally. When we hear them start, which is kind of amazing when you consider that the house is so big, she puts on headphones and colors in her notepad. She seems to have the attitude that what they do or say to each other has nothing to do with her.

Derek's different. He'll sit there and scowl and scowl and scowl.

"Do you want to talk about it?" I'll ask.

"What's to talk about? They're actors. This is what they do."

He's got a point, but I don't want to bad-mouth them in any way—I am starting to love this kid, I'll admit, but I also know he'd sell me out to his parents in exchange for a new video game.

I considered talking to Tess about it—super gently, of course. I planned to say something like "I'm worried about Derek. He seems bothered by something. Do you know what it is?" And hope that she would tell me "Yes, it's probably because Ron and I are fighting. We'll try to keep it quieter."

But as it happened, I didn't need to broach it with Tess. Because Ron broached it with *me*.

Tess has gone with her best friend to Nobu, the sushi restaurant of all sushi restaurants, after another round of afternoon screaming about God-knows-what. I really don't know what, because although I can hear their voices from the kids' wing of the house, I can't hear specific words. I put the kids to bed and was planning to leave, so I checked in with Ron to make sure it was okay.

He was watching Monday Night Football, and drinking a beer. I noticed a few empty bottles on the table in front of him.

"Hey!" he said. "Have a seat. You a football fan?" I told him I was, but that I was just on my way out if he didn't need me.

"Oh." He looked surprised. "Well, maybe just stay a few minutes more, to make sure the kids are asleep? I don't really have the energy to deal with them if it's one of those nights where they have trouble winding down."

"Okay," I said. "Sure." I made a move to go back to the kids' wing, but he reached out and grabbed my arm. Oh my

God. I am definitely a professional, but Ron Powell was *touching* me. The same Ron Powell who, I have to admit, adorned the walls of my room for a brief phase when I was a freshman in high school.

"Take a load off," he said. "Have a beer."

I pondered my options. I couldn't offend him by leaving the room (and didn't want to leave, to be honest). I would stay. But I would be very, very careful. His dimples were dangerous—hundreds of articles in *Cosmo* and *People* and *Us* had said as much.

"A soda sounds great," I said, and grabbed one from the bar. We talked about the game for a few minutes. He seemed to like that I know football quite well. I figured enough time had passed that he would feel comfortable that the kids were sleeping, and was about to take my leave. Whew! Dimples avoided!

That's when he said, "So. I'm sure you've noticed that Tess and I have been fighting a lot lately." He turned to me and his eyes were smoldering. Can eyes do that, though? Obviously not, so how was he doing it?

What to say? *Shit.* I didn't want to embarrass him by saying, "Yep—we pretty much hear everything except your actual words." But I couldn't deny it, because he'd know I was lying. So I gave him a concerned, sympathetic look.

He went on. "Marriage is a tough deal, I'm not going to lie. I love Tess, but it's like I can't do anything right in her eyes. She wants me to take a role and I do. Then she gets mad that

I'm working so much and can't visit her on her set. So I make time to visit her set, and she's mad because my being there was too distracting for people. I mean, what am I supposed to do?"

He's not looking to come on to you, Kirsten, I thought. *Chill. He just needs someone to talk to. Pretend like he's one of your guy friends.*

"I'm sorry," I finally said. "That sounds hard."

"Yeah," he said. "And I know it's hard for the kids. When I grew up, my mom and dad fought all the time, and I hated it. How are they doing?"

I took a breath. Here goes. "I think Ali handles it okay," I said. "But I believe it upsets Derek."

Ron stared at me for a long time, and then blinked. *Was that wrong? Did I say the wrong thing?* Tears sprung to his eyes. He rubbed them with his beautiful, masculine—*oh my God, get ahold of yourself, Kirsten!*—hands.

He cleared his throat. "Thank you," he said. "For listening, for being honest with me. I'm so glad the kids have you in their lives."

Yeah, this was too much. I was in dangerous territory—this man was just too sexy. I stood up to go. "Just doing my job."

He stood up, too, and opened his arms to hug me. *One quick hug, Kirsten. Then you beeline for that door.* I gave him a quick squeeze. Oh my, he smelled so good. Oh my, it felt so good to feel his arms pulling me in.

But I'm no fool. I pulled away after just a second, and said, "Take care, Ron."

Kirsten out. And not yet out of a job. At least, I hoped not.

JEREMY

Is there a sign on my head that says "gigolo" or something? Because if there is I'd like to know about it. Look, I'm no saint, but I'm pretty good to the women I date. I don't mess around on them, and I'm not one to jump into the sack right away. And as far as I can tell, I have never, ever sent a message of availability to Mrs. Black.

You know how I mentioned that she gave me lots of compliments? Yeah, well, now I feel like an idiot. Okay, here's what happened. It started a while ago. The compliments were just the beginning. Then one afternoon, she had a party of girlfriends over to play mahjong or poker or something like that. I was watching Chase, and a couple of the guests' kids. We were doing our thing, and heard the ladies getting louder and louder. They were laughing hysterically and pretty clearly drunk.

"Jeremy!" I heard Mrs. Black call.

As I suspected, the ladies were surrounded by empty wine bottles, their faces flushed, and some of them were about to fall off their chairs.

"Oh, Jeremy, could you be a darling and take the kids swimming? I was just telling everyone about the new basketball hoop we have down in the pool, and we're just sure the kids would love trying it out."

"Okay," I said. I was a little confused, because Mrs. Black pretty much never told me what activity she thought I should do with Chase. "Do the kids all know how to swim pretty well?" I was not about to have four weak swimmers under my watch all at once.

"Yes, absolutely!" a chorus of women shot back at me.

So I changed into my swim trunks, rounded the kids up and into theirs, got us all towels, and down we went to the pool. Have I mentioned how gorgeous this pool is? Like, Olympic-size. Hawaii-resort size. And always heated to the perfect temperature. There was even a waterslide. It sure beat the community pool I'd grown up going to.

We took turns shooting the ball into the hoop, and the kids did really seem to love it. *Good idea, Mrs. Black*, I thought. Then I heard laughing—a lot of it. I looked up and saw the whole mahjong party gathered on the balcony that overlooked the pool. And there was no mistaking the look on Mrs. Black's face. She looked right at me, only me, with lust. Her friends did, too.

I tried to ignore them. I fired off a shot, and though I missed the hoop, the ladies all hooted. WTF? Did they think this was okay with me? Furious, I got out of the pool to their catcalls. In the presence of their children, seriously? Geez, this was ridiculous. I pulled my towel around me, at which point all I heard from above was "Boooo!" "Get back in the pool, Jeremy!" "Come on, Jeremy, we want to see your abs! I mean, we want to see your shots!"

I sat on the side of the pool, ignoring them and playing referee and lifeguard until the women gave up and went inside. But one of them came down to the pool—I think her name was Shirley. For some reason, she had changed into a bikini, and although she didn't look half-bad, it was totally weird and I was really uncomfortable. I kept my distance, but you're not going to believe this: when I rounded up the kids to go inside, she came up behind me and snapped her towel against my ass.

"What the—" I yelled.

"Oops," Shirley smiled. "Sorry."

I definitely had to talk to Mrs. Black about this.

And I did, the next day.

"Yesterday was really embarrassing for me," I said.

"Oh, I know!" she said. "I'm so glad you brought it up; I was just about to. It was embarrassing for me, too—I can't believe my friends acted like that! I promise I will not let them drink that much over here again. Did you know my friend Shelly actually threw up? A grown woman! Outrageous."

And what about you? I thought, but then thought better of saying anything out loud. She got the point.

Then a few weeks later, the house manager calls me and says Mr. and Mrs. Black are separating. They'll send out a press release, but want to keep it quiet for the time being. I can't say I was shocked. I've never seen them together, and when Mrs. Black talks about her husband it's usually with bitterness. I feel sorry for her, I really do. So far as I can tell, the dude is never around. The house manager told me to just stay tuned—my job would change, he thought, but the details were still being worked out.

That very day I got a call from Mrs. Black telling me she needed me over there at once. Technically I was on call, not completely off duty (whoever heard of someone other than a doctor being "on call," by the way? One of the many things that weirds me out about this job sometimes), so I went over expecting that she needed me to take Chase to his guitar lesson or something.

When I got there, the house was quiet. I called out for Chase, but he didn't poke his head out of his room like usual. When I went to his door and knocked, he didn't answer, so I opened it. Empty.

Jazz music was coming from Mrs. Black's wing, so I figured he must be in with her. I knocked on her door.

"Jeremy, is that you?" she said. "Come on in."

I opened the door and saw her sitting on her couch, wearing a silk robe and drinking a glass of wine. The music played softly from a corner of the room, and candles were lit all around the suite.

"Darling, have a seat," she said, and motioned for me to sit in the chair next to the couch. "Can I pour you a glass?"

"I'm okay, thanks. Where's Chase?"

"He's at his friend's house," she said. "I wanted to talk to you alone."

"Oh. Okay."

"I'm sure you heard about Mr. Black and I?"

"Yes," I said. "I'm really sorry to hear it."

"Pshaw." She waved her hand. "It's nothing. It's been coming for years. I can only be his leading lady for so long. I'm sure there's someone younger and prettier waiting to take my spot."

"What are you going to do?" I asked.

"About?"

I could feel my face reddening. "Oh, I don't know. Um, about Chase, about the house, I guess."

"Right," she nodded. "Well, I'm planning to move, actually. To the Palm Springs house. I'll be there full-time."

"And Chase?"

"He doesn't want to leave his school, for what reason I don't know," she said. I was surprised, too. I thought that after the fight and janitor-closet experience, he'd be happy to start somewhere new.

"So I'll be staying here with him?"

"Well, that's the thing," she said. "Any time Chase isn't in school, he'll be with me. Weekends, holidays, summers, everything. So I'd like you to move with me to the Palm Springs house."

I was confused. A live-in position? That wasn't what I wanted, and hadn't been what they wanted. "But what will I do when Chase isn't there?" I asked.

"Oh, you'll still get paid your full salary," Mrs. Black said. "In fact, you'll be making more, since you won't have any living expenses. And I can throw in a raise to sweeten the deal, too."

I'd be paid more to work less? It just didn't make sense. Why would she be offering this to me? I mean, I know I was good with Chase, but to move me to Palm Springs to be his weekend nanny? Wouldn't it make more sense to stay at his primary residence?

"Thank you, Mrs. Black. Can I think about it?"

"Of course," she said. "Please let our house manager know tomorrow. And Jeremy?" She leaned over to me so that I could see her cleavage, touched my arm, and let her fingers linger. "Don't worry—you're worth every penny I'll pay you."

I drove home shaking my head, still confused. My mom was home, drinking coffee and reading the paper in the kitchen, so I slumped down across from her to ask what she made of it all. I told her all the details of the strange afternoon visit. When I finished she looked alarmed.

"Jeremy," she said, and I could tell she was fighting to keep her voice under control, to act like she wasn't freaking out. "That . . . that *woman* . . . that woman wants you to be her boy toy. She wants to pay you to live with her in Palm Springs and be available to her."

"*Mom!*" I shouted. "You're crazy. No way." I stood up and pushed my chair in. But I didn't storm out of the room the way I thought I would. The silk robe, the way she leaned over me at the end—and I hadn't even told my mom that part. Was I an idiot, or just really, really naïve?

I thought about it all night, and the next day I went to see the house manager.

"Here's the deal," I told him, surprised by the firmness in my voice. "I'll stay, but only in Hollywood. I will not go to the Palm Springs house under any circumstances, even if Chase is there. Tell Mrs. Black whatever reason you want, but those are my terms. If they're not acceptable, then I'll submit my resignation. I'm happy to report to you and Mr. Black from now on."

He looked surprised. And, if I wasn't mistaken, a little impressed. "Fine," he said. "I'll let you know."

TRACY

I love Rome. I love everything about it. The trattorias at every corner, the piazzas, the fountains, the ruins, the romance. Yes, the romance. I, Tracy the boring nanny, have met someone. He is not an Italian womanizer—heavens no! He's English, and I met him years ago, when we were both living in London.

I had yesterday off, and Colin was with his mum and dad, so I was free to explore one of my favorite cities. I started with a cappuccino at a café near the Trevi Fountain, where I sat people watching. Only to find out, someone was watching *me*. Tom was at the table right behind me, and (I later learned) debating with himself whether or not to approach me.

"Tracy?" he said. I recognized his squinty blue eyes immediately. He was good friends with some friends of mine in London. I'd quite liked him when we met before, but he'd been dating someone.

"Tom!" I stood to embrace him and offer him the seat across from me. "What a small world! How lovely to see you! I heard you were traveling a lot these days—are you still based in London?"

"No, no," he said. "I'm settled in Rome now."

"Splendid!" I said. He was a banker of some sort, I remembered, and a good one at that. He was tall and a little gangly, and still had the flop of sandy hair that fell over his eyes. He was one of those chaps who just always smiled, and when he smiled, his eyes smiled with him. "I'm here for several weeks myself," I explained, "with the family I work for now."

"You are still nannying then," he replied. "I'd have thought some chap would have whisked you off and married you by now."

I blushed.

"I have the entire day to myself," he said, brushing his hair from his eyes. "Wanna spend it with me? I can be your tour guide!"

We visited all of the spots I'd been eager to see, even though he'd certainly been to them a dozen or more times over. We walked for miles, and when we got tired we stopped for a cappuccino and a snack to refuel. It turned out that he had ended his relationship years before. He didn't expand and I didn't ask him to. The lovely thing about Brits being with Brits, if you ask me, is that we know when to leave well enough alone.

I felt like Audrey Hepburn in *Roman Holiday*. Spending ten hours in this man's company just did something to me. When I popped in to the loo, I saw my reflection in the mirror, and it just proved the point. My skin—usually so pale— was flushed a rosy pink. I usually pull my long brown hair into a bun, and today was no different, but all the walking and lying on the grass had loosened it. I looked soft and happy, which I thought I always had been, but now I looked different and I liked what I saw.

As the day cooled down and night fell, we stopped in to a trattoria that Tom said was his favorite. "You won't believe the gnocchi," he said. He ordered a bottle of wine, which I initially declined as I'm so used to not drinking on the job or off. But tonight I was enjoying a different me and I allowed myself one glass. We drank, ate, and talked. We were from the same neighborhood outside of London, and we caught up on all our favorite spots. We talked about our friends and who was dating whom. We talked about how much we both loved to travel. Moving to Rome was brilliant, he said—he had been itching to get out of England, at least for a while. We talked about all of the other places we wanted to go, and I told him all about Hong Kong, and how good my bosses were to me.

As if on cue, my phone buzzed.

"So sorry to bother you," Cathy said when I picked up. "It's the witching hour, you how that is, and Colin's a little crazy." She just about managed a little laugh. "And so, it appears, are his parents. We seem to have run out of diapers. Where do you keep the extras?"

"No worries at all," I said. "They're under the sink in the laundry room."

"Thanks!" Then she hung up.

Ten minutes later, Mitch called. "Sorry to bother you," he said, "but do you put diaper cream on each time you change Colin's diaper, or just every few times?" He laughed. "Neither Cathy nor I can remember, for some reason."

"I'd go ahead and put it on," I said.

Tom watched these exchanges with amusement, though I was mortified to be answering my phone at dinner.

"I'm surprised they keep calling you when you're off," he said.

I shrugged. "I may be off duty, but I'm always on call."

After dinner, we strolled some more, and when we reached the river, Tom took my hand.

Ring! The bloody phone again.

"Sorry, Tom," I said as I retracted my hand to answer it.

"Oh thank goodness you picked up," Cathy said. "I'm so sorry, but I can't remember how much water we add to Colin's formula."

"It says on the canister," I said, but was careful to keep the edge out of my voice. Because, really! "And Cathy, remember the daily chart, everything is written out on there."

"Right, got it. So sorry!" *Click.*

Tom seemed undeterred, and took my hand once more. "Tracy, I've had such a lovely time with you today. I'd like to see you again while you're here. As much as possible. If you can make that work." He was smiling, as usual, but so shy that he wasn't looking in my eyes.

"I'd love that," I said, and squeezed his hand. We continued walking hand in hand until we found a gelato stand. We got our gelatos; mine was pistachio: green and light and delicious. We sat together on the Tiber River wall, dangling our legs. I felt like a teenager.

It's not like I had never been on a date before. I had lots of boyfriends in London. Well, a few boyfriends, anyway. But it had been a while. I just can't seem to get my head around the American men. And my last serious relationship was . . . well, so long ago that I'm not even sure it's fair to count it. My friends always rib me about it. They say I'm too picky, too wedded to my job, and too buttoned up to let anyone really know me. Truth be told, I didn't even have a really close group of friends anymore—not since England, anyway. I travel too much.

Goodness, all of a sudden this seems so depressing. But I love my life, and the friends I have are wonderful and worth keeping in touch with. As for my romantic life, I always knew I'd know him when I met him. And now I think I might have.

LAURA

Men are gross.

Seriously gross.

It's not like I hate *all* men. I just have a very specific type that I'm interested in. I like guys who are creative, a little artsy. Good dressers. Totally comfortable talking about their feelings. The kind of guys who seem maybe even gay, until you get alone in a room with them and then—*whoa!*—definitely not gay. But my main requirement is that they be UNDER forty-five!

My *dad* is forty-five. *Stephen Colbert* is forty-five (at least). I am twenty-two, and I am not at all interested in someone who is forty-five.

Lillian has been driving me crazy. She's become obsessed with setting me up with this friend of James's. His name is Chris and he and James went to college together and are pretty close. Lillian's known him for years, too. He's a handsome guy, but totally not my type. He's a guy's guy, all into sports and cars and macho things that just don't interest me at all. Plus he's *forty-five!*

I guess he said something to Lillian about finding me attractive and she won't leave it alone. She teases me, saying things like "Wear something nice at dinner tonight—Chris is coming!" I told her flat out that I wasn't interested, but she didn't seem to hear me. "Trust me, Laura," she said. "I know a thing or two about men, and Chris is one of the good ones."

"I don't doubt that, Lillian," I said, "but that doesn't change the fact that he's not my type, and that he's your friend, which in my book puts him off-limits."

"Laura!" she laughed. "Obviously I don't care if you see him. You're just being silly. And you think you have a type, but if you're open, you might see that you can fall for someone completely against type. You know, James wasn't my type at all. But he's perfect for me."

She had a point. James didn't seem to be her type. He was too down-home Midwest, and she was all LA. In this case, though, it was Chris's age that really made for a nonstarter, but I couldn't say that to her because she might get offended. She was probably forty-two, maybe older. I learned you can never really trust how old Wikipedia says someone is; people in Hollywood know how to game that system.

"Lillian, leave her alone," James barked. He was making himself a sandwich in the kitchen while we played with the kids in the living room. "I don't want Chris near Laura. You don't know him as well as I do."

"But James—"

"Seriously, Lillian. What would Laura's parents think of her bosses trying to set her up?"

I flushed a little at James's reference to my parents, but was also kind of glad he made it. It seemed Lillian needed to be reminded of my age. And that she was my employer.

She dropped it then, but I noticed that Chris stopped by the house more frequently, sometimes when James wasn't there. I couldn't help but think Lillian had invited him. What was her angle? Why did she even want me to date him? I couldn't figure it out. Part of me thought maybe she was attracted to Chris, and needed somewhere for that energy to go. But a bigger part of me thought she wanted it because if I were with Chris, she could control me more.

Ugh, I know how that sounds. It sounds a bit like *The Hand That Rocks the Cradle* obsession stuff, but I don't mean to be that dramatic about it. I just mean that Lillian likes calling the shots in my life. She asks to see my schedule of classes so she can weigh in and let me know whether or not the time slots work for her. If she thinks my course load will be too challenging, she tells me so, and reminds me she doesn't want me to be tired or distracted at work. She asks me questions about my love life, which I am always ducking.

Then she went a step too far. We were at a big beach party thrown by one of Lillian and James's friends. My presence had been required, she said, because the kids were coming, too, and she didn't want to have to keep tabs on them the whole evening. She came over to where I was playing with them and some other kids on the sand, and told me to take a break, that she wanted to watch them by herself for a bit—I'd had to pee for ages and took her up on the offer with some relief. When I returned about ten minutes later, Lillian was there, but the kids weren't.

"They're tired. Billy pulled the car up," she said, referring to the limo driver they used sometimes. "They're waiting for you out front. Can you take them home, please?"

"Sure thing," I said, and dusted the sand off my feet on my way to the car. It was waiting in front of the beachside mansion, just as Lillian said, and I opened the side door and hopped in. The limo took off immediately, and when I turned around, I saw that the kids were not in their usual seats in the back.

"What the h—" I started to say, and the window partition came down so I could see there was someone in the front passenger seat. It was Chris.

"What's going on?" I asked. "Where are the kids?"

He laughed. "Still at the party," he said. "They didn't want to go home yet. It was a ruse. Lillian thought you deserved a night off. Surprise!"

Surprise.

"So where would you like to go?" he asked amiably.

I hated her for this. I'd never had a creepy vibe from Chris, but Lillian knew I wasn't interested. What was Lillian doing pimping out her nanny? At the very least, she had put me in an incredibly awkward position. Whenever I saw him from now on, it would be uncomfortable for me, and uncomfortable for him.

So I did the only thing I could think of to do. I lied. "Oh gosh!" I said. "That's so nice of Lillian! She doesn't know this, but it's my boyfriend's birthday today. I was planning to meet up with him later, but if the driver wouldn't mind dropping me off with him now, that would be the greatest surprise ever."

"Oh . . . sure . . . ," he said. "Um, okay. Where does he live?"

I thought fast and gave him my friend Sam's address. I prayed that Sam would play along, that he'd be there and his boyfriend wouldn't be, or that the limo would just drop me off in front. I also prayed that my gut feeling about Chris was sort of right and he wasn't the jealous type. Sam was definitely not capable of defending himself.

We drove along quietly for a while, and then Chris said, "Lillian didn't mention you have a boyfriend."

"Yeah, that makes sense. She doesn't know. I'm not trying to keep it from her or anything," I added quickly. "I just try to keep it professional at work, you know?"

Do you know, Chris? Do you hear what I'm telling you?

"Right," he said.

I texted Sam:

Me: "I'm headed to your house. Play along, please."

Sam: "???"

Me: "I'll tell you later. Just please. Okay, bf?"

Sam: "???"

I sighed. We clearly needed a code for when my boss has me kidnapped for a date that I don't want to go on and I am using him for an out. Because something told me this wouldn't be the last time Lillian pulled a stunt like this.

CHAPTER FOUR

· · · · · · · · · · · · · · · · · · ·

The Luxury

Nanny Wears Prada

Hollywood, as a town and lifestyle, begs all who come near it to enjoy it. Hollywood invites passersby to be open to its gilded charms and its promise of new personas and more money than one could possibly spend. Hollywood promises an overnight fix for almost anything that ails one's self-esteem. Hollywood tells people they can paint away their flaws, they can buy a new reflection, and if all fails they can borrow, or build for themselves, the lifestyle of the rich and famous, simply by being close to a celebrity—maybe even by being their nanny.

QUESTION: What do designer clothes, five-star-hotel gourmet room service, Manolo Blahniks, million dollar homes, plus more Prada than you know what do with all have in common?

ANSWER: For those slow on the uptake, the common factor here is not the celebrity's lifestyle, it's the personal lifestyle of their *nanny*. These days, nannies don't just enjoy the proximity of their bosses' successes; they are up close and personal with their own.

CAN I *DRIVE* IT?

One of Stella's first big gifts was a TV, which her employers gave her for her birthday. It was a 55-inch Sony that she called Bertha. When the digital engineer came to install Bertha, he mentioned that it was a $15,000 television, and Stella choked on her tea.

"You're fucking joking, aren't you?" she said. And he said, "No. Why?"

"You see that car out there? That didn't cost $15,000. Who spends $15,000 on a TV? I can't drive it, I can't wear it on my finger, and it doesn't do the dishes." He looked at her as if she were an idiot. Not to take anything away from the wonderful, generous gifts families give, but they are often gifts appropriate to the parents' world, not the nanny's.

The nanny grows comfortable with being a super-consumer because she has played the role so many times on behalf of her boss. It's not uncommon when the kids are in school that nanny will be sent to Rodeo Drive to do her boss's bidding. The sales associates look bewildered until she flashes a black American Express, and asks for one of everything in their spring collection . . . size 2, please. Sizing her up, the sales associate surmises that she's clearly not a 2. Nanny is only human. Despite the fact the clothes aren't for her, she relishes the attention, particularly when she's asked if she'd like a double mocha cappuccino (they can tell she likes the high-calorie stuff!) or hears, "Shall we call out for a sandwich from Jerry's Deli while you shop?" Of course she slips happily into the Manolos of her client's life, even if it's for just a moment. "Yes," she answers to the sandwich question, with a little more grandeur than she had three hours ago when she was elbow-deep in making school lunches. "Tuna salad please, on rye." And now she's hooked.

There's no doubt that working for a Hollywood celebrity is a wonderful way to live a first-class lifestyle. One of Julie's nannies spent three months in Malta, then two years traveling around Europe, followed by six months in London. Most families, because they have such great help, will take their kids with them for extended lengths of time. Families have second and third homes in exotic locations, and the nannies are often invited to vacation there themselves, and sometimes even invite their own families and friends. We know one nanny who travels to her bosses' multimillion dollar home in Aspen every summer for her two-week vacation, and she takes about ten friends. Sort of brilliant, really.

NANNY LIVES VICARIOUSLY

Stella's been to a Lakers game twice in her life. The first time was in the nosebleed section; the second was court-side where the tickets cost $2,200 each, and her date was a six-year-old.

She has a watch collection that totals approximately $10,000, and a bag collection that includes a vintage Hermès Kelly bag from 1964. She's flown on private planes to the most exclusive destinations in the world, been on vacations and had dinners with the who's who of Hollywood, and been to movie premieres that some would sacrifice limbs for.

On a daily basis she was cooked for by a private chef, had her bed made by the housekeeper, and was spun around Beverly Hills by a driver. She enjoyed those mind-blowing gifts and experiences at the hands of wonderful, generous people that she was nanny for.

Beyond the travel, nanny gets first dibs on her boss's cast-off designer outfits. There are also stupendous bonuses at Christmas. In one household, every staff member, including the housekeepers, had to make a list of ten items they wanted for Christmas (and the family was Jewish!). The only rule: everything on the list had to be $1,000 or over. The nanny thought, okay, great, she'd get one of these ten things and would be delighted. She made her list and gave it to the PA, and wondered what she would be opening on Christmas morning—because, of course, she'd be working. She was floored, amazed, shocked, and a bit embarrassed when she started collecting things from around the tree that had her name on them. They had bought her everything on the list. Ten thousand dollars of gifts for each of their staff. The nanny was gobsmacked.

Another nanny, Sheila from North Dakota, got a gold keychain from Tiffany from her Saudi royal family bosses one day, and the very next day they gave her a diamond watch. The nanny felt uncomfortable, it was all too much, and tried to give it back. "No," the family's mum said. "The watch is a gift from the children, and they wouldn't understand why you couldn't take it." Oh, well. If you insist!

These stories really just touch the surface. As one nanny told us, "Working as a celebrity nanny is strange, because however much you love kids, they end up coming second to the life itself. Taking care of the children becomes a by-product of living the lavish life they are part of."

Remember that drug awareness campaign, showing what drugs do to your brain? "This is your brain," says a voice, holding up a pristine egg. Then it's cracked into a frying pan where it sizzles away as the voice says, "This is your brain on drugs." Well, imagine now that instead of being cracked into a frying pan, that lovely egg is hard-boiled and peeled, wrapped in sausage, battered, and deep-fried—the Scotch egg of our homeland. *That* is your brain on wealth.

The American Dream is all about accumulating wealth and assets. So there is nanny, driving her fancy car around Beverly Hills. Her Prada bag is beside her and her Louis Vuitton sunglasses block the California sun. She thinks she's made it, that she's achieved the American Dream. What she's forgetting is that, although she has accumulated this stuff, the lifestyle is borrowed. At some point she will choose to leave, or she will be sacked. If she hasn't saved, she will have to sell that Prada bag and those Louis Vuitton sunglasses. She will have to wait in line at theme parks and restaurants. Not only will she have to fly commercial, she'll have to fly economy.

This is a system that truly does fuck with you, pardon our French. If nanny is fired, she feels she's lost a huge part of herself that she had no time to adjust to. She will have lost her identity. We've seen many nannies go through this, and it's really like a death. We apologize if this section reads a bit like it's from a self-help book, but there is a price to be paid for the glitzy life of a Hollywood celebrity nanny.

TRAVELING, CELEBRITY-STYLE

Two nannies offered testimonials of life on the road with their celebrity families:

Bridget: I can't believe summer is here again and we're embarking on twelve weeks of travel! I go through a last-minute checklist of my personals: Chanel bag . . . check. Balenciaga purse . . . check. Tod's loafers . . . check. Prada carry-on . . . check. Louis Vuitton wallet for euros . . . check. TechnoMarine watch . . . check. It's not all going to be vacation for my boss, as there will be a lot of press junkets for the latest blockbuster.

The flight is great; flying private is always such a treat. When I was growing up we didn't have a lot of money, but ever since I've had this life, I've only known VIP treatment.

We land in the south of France—Nice, to be precise, and continue on by car and driver to the hotel. Who knew that little old me from a town in the middle of nowhere would end up living like this? I've been with this family for eight years and we're still happy with one another.

We arrive at the Hôtel du Cap-Eden-Roc, about which the following has been written: "[It] has become a mystical refuge whose history blends in with that of the celebrities who come from the [four] corners of the world to find their part of paradise: luxury in all its simplicity." We're greeted by the staff, people who have known us for years. They are fully at our disposal to meet our expectations and enhance our comfort.

After a while, we head down to our private cabana and the children and I do some serious frolicking in the pool. Back at our suite, I call room service. Jean-Jacques, our private butler, is on a break, but a lovely lady takes my order. At the end she says, "Merci, Madame Bernstein." I pause, just imagining for a moment I was the Madame; then reality hits and I reply with a laugh, "Oh, no, this isn't Madame Bernstein, this is Bridget, the nanny!"

Siobhan: I was horrified when the limo driver asked me for my passport on the way to the airport. *Oh my God*, I thought, *what's he wanting with my private papers?* When we rolled onto the tarmac at Santa Monica airport, I was amazed to see a plane just feet from the car, a private little jet of a plane. I shuttled the kids out, trying to look like this was an everyday event for me (yeah, right!). With mom, kids, and bags all safely onboard, I checked the limo one more time for favorite toys, blankets, etc. The driver appeared and almost shocked me to kingdom come when he said, "Here's your passport. You're all set for customs." *No way!*

I replied, "No lines, no nothing?"

"No, no lines," the driver said, looking at me strangely.

Then I looked around to make sure no one could hear, and asked with all my sweet Irish naïveté, "So where do the planes come from? Do you dial them up, like 1-800 plane?" He laughed at what he thought was a joke . . . which it wasn't, but I was too embarrassed to admit it!

We always warn the nannies who take the highest pro-file positions—the ones with the largest salaries and the most demanding bosses: "You're not going to have time for a life of your own. Do you understand that?" The nannies nod up and down like those dashboard dolls, but they don't believe us. Or they do believe us, but they don't care. They are willing to give up their lives completely. Fine, they've made that choice. But once they've done so, once they've forsaken their former selves, can they ever walk away? Because, you see, they've got nothing left. It is not uncommon for nannies to get all sorts of wiggy at the end of their journey through stardom . . . unless they marry the star, of course (see chapter three: "The Sex"). It's hard—really hard—when she leaves her job and her bor-rowed oh-so-important persona leaves with it. Once nanny has had the press hiding outside her house, following her and the kids to school, and her mum calling to say she saw a pic-ture of nanny in the *National Enquirer*, slipping back to nor-malcy can and does feel dull, at best.

The nanny is also in financially dangerous territory, espe-cially if she's become too caught up in the lifestyle. Nothing makes that point clearer than this testimonial by a sad case, Melissa, who was financially ruined when she lost her job: "I don't know what happened. Sometimes I blame my now ex-fiancé and his expensive tastes. I blame myself for not plan-ning better, and when I'm not blaming either of us, I find myself thinking I should have been paid more. I know that's just silly, because I would have just spent more, and bought a bigger house. At the peak of my nanny career I was making a minimum of $600 a day, plus a per diem which I never used. I drove a Mercedes and bought my then-boyfriend a truck . . . just because I could. We bought a three-story house that was listed at almost a million dollars. The mortgage wasn't an issue as I was making so much, and I put some cash down when we bought it.

"To this day I don't know why I thought we needed a six-thousand-square-foot house just for the two of us and our cat. I was never planning on having kids. Cut to now, and I'm broke. I'm filing for bankruptcy next week. I didn't think ahead. Didn't consider what I'd do if things changed. I've never struggled to find work, either in the US or South Africa, where I'm from. Now the car has gone, the keys to the house went back to the mortgage company two months ago, and my ex left and took the truck . . . the only thing I paid cash for. I'm so depressed that I'm struggling to even get to interviews. Oh my God, why didn't I save? I just can't believe I let so much money slip through my hands."

Let's not forget that there's a cost when nanny's actually *in* the job, too. Luxury has a flip side for those dispensing it. Nanny may be asked to wear a uniform, in which case she has become a status symbol, there to be seen but not heard. She may be expected to know the parents' needs before even they or their personal assistants know what they want. She may be expected to fly coach with screaming kids wanting their mommies—mommies who are sequestered away in first class sipping on Dom and reading about themselves in *Vanity Fair*. She may be on call 24-7 when traveling. In addition to vacations, she will probably also work the holidays . . . and yes, we mean all the holidays, including the Lord's birthday (and no, we're not religious!).

"As a nanny you have to be careful about what glitters, because it's not always gold," said manny Alex. "When you're a celebrity nanny, yes, there are wonderful perks, like whole art-project closets, not just drawers; libraries of great children's books, not just bookshelves; a pool in the backyard, not down the street; travel by private jet, not by minivan; and salaries that are not just competitive, but the highest. Beyond all the glamour, though, be sure that the family you work for respects a nanny's role in their lives and the lives of their children. Unfortunately, if you are just another cog in their wheel, no amount of money, planes, pools, or canvas art supplies will make the really long days go faster!"

Herewith, our favorite "You can't pay me enough or give me enough perks to do this job!" stories:

JANELLE: Was awakened at three o'clock in the morning with mum carrying a tired-looking three-year-old. "She wants to play hide-and-seek," mum chuckled through her red wine–stained lips. "Are you kidding me?" Janelle wanted to say, but instead heard herself reply sleepily, "Yes, of course, let's play a little hide-and-seek." (On call 24-7. We mentioned that, right?)

OUT OF HER DEPTH

Not every nanny is cut out for the glamour and the travel. A lot of American girls, in particular, aren't used to traveling, and why would they be when they live in a country where they can ski and surf all in the same day? They sometimes get very overwhelmed. Julie had a nanny call crying from Paris. She was staying with the family at George V, one of the fanciest hotels in all of the city, and the mum had given her $500 to take the kids around town for the day. The nanny didn't speak French, hadn't traveled much before, and she was afraid of taking the underground. *Bloody hell*, Julie thought. *Stop whining and make it work!*

Another seasoned but new-to-the-celebrity-circuit nanny, let's call her Andrea, called in a panic because when she sat down to a formal dinner in a chateau in Tuscany, she didn't know how to use silverware the European way. The parents and their friends frowned at her, and one of the children laughed and pointed as Andrea cut her food with her knife all at once, only to lay it down and begin eating with her fork in her right hand. "I'm so embarrassed," she sobbed in the phone.

"For God's sake," Julie told her, "that's what YouTube is for! Get online and make sure you're holding a knife and fork at all times moving forward." Within a couple of days, she was an expert!

AMY: Was asked not to speak directly to the parents unless they spoke to her first. All comments or questions had to first go through the personal assistant, just to make sure that it was worth the parents hearing. She also had to fold down their beds at night, and put a little candy on their pillow. *Seriously, people!*

WENDY: Was forbidden to speak to the celebrity father when he was in rehearsals, as were the rest of the family and staff. Something about not wanting to strain his voice. She had to write messages from the kids and the mum on Post-it notes and leave them lined up on his desk. (No, guys, this wasn't TC. It was some B-list actor from one of the daytime soaps who had no more than a dozen lines per week!)

SAM: Had to double as a uniformed waitress when the family had friends over for dinner, and was required to learn formal service . . . *formal service!*

TYLER: Had to accompany his boss, a single mom, to any and all social functions. She bought him designer clothes, had a barber come to the house to cut and style his hair and shave him (shave his *face*—come on now, this is a family book!). Not so bad, you think? Well, not until he had to attempt to get her worse-for-wear ass to bed at three o'clock in the morning, and then wake his own ass up three hours later to be with the kids!

And then there's the other dark side of fame and luxury, one that would-be celebrity nannies surely never think about when applying for the job: the paparazzi.

Here's Emily's story:

"I work for a celebrity, but sometimes I feel like I am one because of all the attention I receive. The lifestyle at work is different from anything I have ever experienced before. I knew celebrities enjoyed opulence, and I knew they lived carefree, but it isn't until you are immersed that you really grasp the magnificence. When I was offered this job, I felt like I had won the lottery! With this position came a significant raise, a brand new SUV, and much-needed health insurance. I was on cloud nine.

"A month after starting, I was informed that we would be going to New York for a few days. I love to travel, so was really excited. Celebrities travel differently than other people. A well-known person doesn't wait in any lines, because that would result in a huge mob scene. The car service with the family's regular driver came to the house to pick us up. When the car pulled up to the airport drop-off curb, a person was there, waiting to escort us to the ticket counter. We didn't have to have contact with anyone else at the airport. Our 'meet-and-greet' person took our driver's licenses and got our tickets for us. Then he carried our bags and we bypassed all lines to go directly through security.

"This was my first experience with paparazzi. At the ticket counter we turned around to start walking toward security, and a huge crowd had formed. Each person had a big camera and was shouting my boss's name. Flashes were everywhere and hundreds of people who were waiting to get through security were now staring and pointing. We had to just try to get through all the cameras because there was only one way to go. The press walks backwards, right in front of you, so you feel like you'll trip at any moment. I was trying not to run into anyone who was standing in line as we maneuvered our way to the front. With the lights, the shouts, the people staring, the cameras, trying to hold on to my carry-on bag and a five-year-old was a gladiator feat. I felt a hot rush of tears trying to break the surface. Luckily, I held them back and my inner actor took over to make sure I looked calm. Except for a few minutes in the airport lounge, we were in public the whole time, so every word and movement elicited stares and double takes from hundreds of people. I have never enjoyed being the center of attention, so being with someone who is gawked at made me feel a little crazy."

Walking Away from the Nanny Underbelly

Post on a nanny website:

Can't really say where this question is coming from but let's say you were approached and given this question—your answer would be?

Listen- you will make 6 figures, be live in for 2 weeks- live out for 2 weeks. When you're 'on' you will be treated like utter sh$@, you will be blamed for things beyond your control, yelled at, degraded, publicly humiliated, run yourself to the point of exhaustion. The kids will be GREAT- but everything else about your job will be HARD- testing everything you've got. No one will appreciate you, and you will run like nuts from 6am-10:30pm with zero breaks. BUT: in your days off u can live like a queen from your earnings. You can pay your bills, and take 2 weeks to recover before you head back into hell. Your doctor will tell you that your hair is falling out due to stress, and your body will hate the crazy schedule you work. But THAT'S the job. WHAT would YOU say to that?

Stella has always prided herself on staying true to herself and her values. But that doesn't mean she doesn't still love caviar. She misses its appearance as part of her working life, preferably with crème fraîche, please. Oh, she misses lobster. Now she could certainly buy and cook a lobster if she wanted to, it's not that expensive. But that's just the thing— she'd have to cook it herself, and what a nightmare! When she sees People magazine now, she gets a little wistful. She used to know the gossip before it hit print. She would hear it over a mealtime conversation, that such-and-such is so happy or such-and-such is breaking up. (Celebrities are friends with celebrities, you know.) She even recognized some of the exotic island location photos, as she'd been there, too, albeit behind the scenes.

And then there were the nanny jobs Stella interviewed for when a famous person was having a baby and starting the quest for a Mary Poppins. She knew her family would love to hear the latest! But no way, that NDA was signed and sealed, and anyway, mum's the word. She was part of the Nanny Underbelly, but at the end of the day, she's still a girl from the North of England who is as content to make her own shepherd's pie—plenty of Lea & Perrins, please—and who really doesn't mind getting her news a few days after it happens.

Even so, there were times when Stella was working as a celebrity nanny when she forgot herself. On occasion it took her brother to bring her back. He lives in London, but often visited Stella in the States, and on one such visit they traveled to New York. They wanted to go to the top of the Empire State Building, but when they got there, the queue wound all around the block. Stella told him, "I'm not standing in this line. I'm going to go see if there's a fast track."

"Cool your jets, Stella," her brother said. "Who do you think you are? Beyond standing in line now, are you?"

Stella couldn't stop her eyes roaming for a fast track. She knew there was a fast track, there are *always* fast tracks. The families she worked for never had to wait for anything. She started asking around, and her brother got embarrassed. He told her she was being pushy and rude, and teased her as only a brother can about how she'd changed. And he was right.

But Stella was right, too. There was a fast track. Stella found a guy carrying a credit card machine around, and he said that they could pay to go to the front of the line. Stella's brother whipped out his credit card in an instant.

All of this luxury boils down to one central question for dear nanny: Can she make like Mary Poppins and blow away when the wind is right?

Stella always knew she could walk away if and when she needed to. That doesn't mean she didn't honor her commitment to the family or love the children. She would have been heartbroken if they had left her life entirely. But she always knew she had her own husband, her own house, her own life, and she wanted those things more than any luxury beach house or five-star hotel room.

Once she was working in Europe with one of her favorite families. They were staying in a magnificent villa. Stella was heading home, but the family was staying a while longer. The dad, whom Stella loved to death, teasingly said, "Why are you so excited to go back to your little mud hut?" He wasn't being intentionally mean—it was his way of letting her know he didn't want her to leave.

"What you don't get," Stella said, "is that it's *my* little mud hut." The point being, as fantastic as this place was, it wasn't hers. It wasn't even her vacation. Despite how wonderful and fabulous everything was, she was still working, and it was time for her to go home.

KIRSTEN

I'm in a groove now, thank God. I managed to avoid Ron for months after what I've come to think of as The Hug, Tess never learned (at least, to my knowledge) that we shared a "moment," and I think the two of them are getting along better. At least, the yelling has diminished. I feel like I'm over the hump and finally able to relish the perks. And let me tell you, *there are perks*. The beautiful home, the beautiful view, the special treatment at Disneyland? That was nothing compared to what lay ahead.

One day in November, Tess called me on my way to work and suggested I go to the family's storage facility instead—the house manager, Sasha, would meet me there. Tess was very mysterious about the whole thing, so naturally I thought I was going to be fired. Instead, when I pulled up, Sasha was sitting outside with a huge smile on her face. When I walked over to her, she handed me a bundle of plastic garbage bags.

"What's this?" I asked.

"We get to go shopping. You can take whatever will fit in your car." With that, she opened the door and I saw the storage facility for the first time. It was huge—the size of the Trader Joe's near my house, if not bigger. While some of it was furniture, most was clothes. Beautiful, beautiful clothes. Expensive clothes. Glorious clothes. *Yes, please.*

I looked at Sasha to see if she was as stunned as I was, but apparently she'd done this before. She had a garbage bag opened and was going through the first rack of shoes.

"Do we all get to do this? Where are Penny and Trish?" I asked, referring to the cook and housekeeper.

"Yeah, they'll come later, after work," she said. "But we get first dibs. I've only got a half an hour before I have to be back at the house." The message was clear: Kirsten, please shut up and let me pillage!

So that was the first hidden perk of the job. I stuffed ten bags with sweaters, dresses, coats, shoes, and even lingerie into my car. I felt so gluttonous. I decided I'd donate some of it. But first I needed to spend time trying it all on in the quiet of my crappy apartment.

My apartment had become a sore point with me. It was charmless. With my new salary, I'd acquired a few nice pieces of furniture, but the walls they sat within were completely blah. I drove a pretty nice car, an Audi—also courtesy of my salary—and began to worry more and more about it getting stolen. My neighborhood in Palms had nothing going for it. I was spending more and more time in Santa Monica, walking along the beach and looking for a new apartment to rent. When I found "the one" a few days after the storage shopping spree, I didn't care what it cost. I mean, I *cared*, but it was worth it. The closet was big enough to house my new clothes.

The garage was secure enough for my car. And the ocean I'd become so accustomed to looking at all day became within my reach at night as well. I am making good money; I deserve to spend it. My parents cautioned me about saving some of it, but I'm in my twenties! There's plenty of time to be practical. For the time being, I just wanted to be *alive*.

Then one day in late December, as if to put an exclamation point on my new lease on life, Tess said she needed to talk to me about the Oscars.

Wow, I thought. *Why is she planning so far ahead? It's over two months away.* The buzz around town was that both she and Ron would be nominated. I knew that in all likelihood I'd have to work that night. But she didn't need to reserve my time that far ahead—she knew that. If I had a *day's* notice, I considered myself lucky.

I didn't say any of this, of course. Tess was just smiling at me, and I wondered what it was she was looking for. Reassurance that she'd be nominated? I had no clue.

"We'll have a hair stylist, makeup artist, and wardrobe people over that day," Tess continued. "But we need to start talking about outfits before then. Can you come up to the house this weekend so we can get started?"

I imagined all my weekend plans falling away one at a time. *She wants me to come in on my day off, months before the Oscars, so I can watch the kids while she tries on dresses!* I forced a smile. *This is what you signed on for.* I reminded myself of my new apartment. "Of course. What day will work for you?"

"Let's say Saturday," she said. "Because the kids will be at soccer camp."

"Wait," I said. "I'm confused. If the kids are going to be at soccer camp, why do you need me?"

Tess laughed her tinkly Hollywood laugh. "*Kirsten*," she said, "we have to decide what you'll wear. All of the nannies who have ever worked with us go to the Oscars. I thought you knew that!"

My first thought was, *How would I know that?* But my much more powerful second thought was, *Ohmygod, ohmygod, ohmygod! I'm going to the Oscars!*

Needless to say, I showed up at the appointed time on Saturday and Tess and I had a fitting with her designer of choice. On Oscar day, I got my hair and makeup done. My brother—whom I invited as my plus-one—and I got to ride in the limo with Tess and Ron, and pretend like we were movie stars when we got out of the car, just like we'd done when we were kids. Only this time, our props were a tad bit more convincing.

Tess and Ron left for home right after the show (neither of them won that year), but said I could take the limo to the *Vanity Fair* party if I wanted. *If I wanted!?!* I danced with George Clooney! Well, not really, but I did dance close to him.

After the party, the limo dropped my brother off first. It was three o'clock in the morning, and I'll never forget the way he looked at me when he got out of the car. "Nice work, sis," he said. "You made it."

JEREMY

I did not get fired for refusing to be Mrs. Black's sex toy.

I stayed on at Mr. Black's insistence, which surprised me because I didn't even think the guy knew my name. Maybe he just didn't want to hassle with finding another manny while also dealing with the divorce.

What surprised me even more was that I started to see Mr. Black at the house once in a while. Not *often*, but, like, once every couple of weeks. He even wanted me and Chase to come out to New York with him for a few days on one of his trips there. I asked the house manager if I'd heard correctly—I'd never seen Mr. Black so interested in his kid that he wanted him along on a business trip.

That was the first time I'd flown on a private plane. I tried to play it cool. Chase didn't seem particularly impressed that we had our own screening room aboard, as well as what amounted to the contents of my mom's entire kitchen at our disposal.

Mr. Black was on the plane with us, busy making calls and doing whatever it was Mr. Black did. It was only on the descent that he came and sat with me and Chase. I'd taught

Chase how to play chess, and we were in the middle of a game where I was whupping his butt. I knew this kid so well, though, that I was monitoring the curl of his lip, the snort of his nostrils, the flush of his skin. It was good to push him a little, and help him learn to control himself in increments. If he got too agitated, though, I'd move on to another activity. I didn't want him losing his shit in front of Mr. Black, especially the only time I'd seen his dad making a (sort of) effort.

Mr. Black sipped his Scotch and regarded our chess board carefully. "Hmm," he said, rubbing his lower lip.

Chase moved his pawn within striking distance of my rook. Mr. Black made a pained face—*wrong move, Chase*—but Chase didn't see it. This put me in a bad place. Should I show Mr. Black I'm a smart guy and understand the game? Or protect Chase from embarrassment by pretending I didn't catch his bad move? These are not normally the strategies of chess, but they were for this game.

Thank God the flight steward came over and interrupted us. "Mr. Black," he said, giving a little bow. "The pilot has instructed me to take my seat for landing in a moment. Is there anything you need before I do?"

"Yeah, could you check the traffic going into Manhattan?"

"Yes, sir, of course."

A moment later, he was back with the report that the traffic was not good.

"Figures," huffed Mr. Black. "Alright, just have a helicopter pick us up from the airport to take us to the apartment."

"Excellent, sir, right away."

Sure, right, I thought. *Because what else would one do when faced with traffic? Call the helicopter!* The helicopter arrived just a few minutes after our wheels touched down, and lifted us over the lights of Manhattan.

As I looked down on the traffic—which truly did look gnarly—I thought about the last time I'd seen New York, when I'd left. Even though I had all my crap with me, I'd taken the subway to Penn Station, then took New Jersey Transit to Newark airport. I'd flown coach back to LA, of course, in a middle seat in the very back, near the bathroom. Good times.

Worse than the way I'd left, though, was *why* I'd left. I couldn't make enough to keep a roof over my head and put food in my belly between paychecks. Why should New York just be a place for the rich and privileged? It wasn't right. Why did Mr. Black get to call a helicopter to move over traffic when, back in LA, my mom was up at five o'clock each day battling her commute? They both worked hard. They both were smart. All of a sudden, the expansive differences between them struck me as plain ludicrous. And for some reason, all of this just made me mad at New York.

New York was a great city, a city I'd loved, but it was also a city that had rejected me. It had chewed me up and spat me out, and now I was back . . . in a helicopter, you motherfuckers!

TRACY

In all my jobs I've done my utmost to keep my private life private; it's a personal rule. If I started dating someone, I was really careful about telling the family I was working for. Much better to let them find out after six or more months, when they can see that I'm managing to see someone without disrupting their lives at all. I know more than one nanny friend who has been let go after telling the parents she has a new boyfriend or has started an evening or weekend class.

I wouldn't have said anything in this case, either, except that Mitch and Cathy pulled me aside and asked me if I might like to go to the opera Saturday night. They had been given two excellent seats by someone on their film crew, but they knew they'd be too tired and thought I might like to go instead.

"I'd love it," I said.

"And you don't mind going alone?" Cathy asked.

"Oh no, but . . . well, I wonder . . . you're not planning to use the second ticket?"

"No, why? Do you have a friend in town?" Mitch asked, and raised an eyebrow. I didn't want to be too cagey with them, or it would seem like I was hiding something. Their imagination would be much worse than the truth. So I told them about Tom, how we'd run into each other at a café, and how I'd seen him a bit during my downtime. I didn't mention we spent *all* of our free time together, that in fact Tom had been spending nearly every night at the flat Mitch and Cathy had rented for me. I wasn't trying to keep it a secret, and they'd never said I couldn't have guests over; I just wanted to keep my life my own.

"That's so wonderful!" Cathy said. "We're delighted you have a companion here in Rome. Absolutely, Tom should take the ticket. And I know the perfect place for you two to have dinner beforehand." She started to jot it down for me, then said, "Wait, no—I'll make you a reservation myself!" I had to chuckle at the role reversal although I stifled my giggle in a cough.

On the night of the opera, Tom looked drop-dead gorgeous in his tuxedo when he picked me up at the flat. He brought a bouquet of red roses for me—my favorite, but it also seemed like the opera thing to do. I loved them.

The restaurant was perfect, as Cathy had said. It was tiny, made of stone, on the outside covered with vines, and on the inside lit up with hundreds of candles and a blazing stone fireplace.

"You are friends with signora Cathy," our waiter announced when he came to our table. "*Per favore* she would like you to have-a your dinner. We have the lovely things prepared." It wasn't clear, with his accented English, what exactly he was saying, but I was pretty sure that Cathy and Mitch were buying our meal. In lieu of a menu, our waiter came over and opened what, judging by the taste, I can only guess was a very expensive bottle of wine. He followed it with *salumi, burrata* with almond and arugula, pappardelle with octopus, and delicious sirloin steak. *Limoncello* followed the meal, plus tiramisu, of course, and espresso. There is no other way to describe the meal other than exquisite. It was the finest food to grace my palate in years.

I'd gone out to nice restaurants with Mitch, Cathy, and Colin before, but I'd always been very cautious about what I ordered. To me, the amounts charged were outrageous, and I never wanted to come across as though I felt entitled. I would often order a simple salad or pasta dish, though they urged me to order whatever I liked. It just didn't seem proper.

But now I was full to the brim and felt warmed, from the inside out. Tom and I linked arms on the short walk to the Teatro dell'Opera, and I was floored as we were led to our box seats.

"You have very generous employers," Tom said, not for the first time that night. I nodded. I felt like the luckiest nanny in all the world. I had a darling child to look after, kind and understanding employers, and culture and love surrounding me. I could have had a normal life working in a nursery school, lived closer to family, had predictable hours, and perhaps joined a book club that I could actually count on being able to attend—but I would have missed out on all of this. It wasn't even a fair comparison.

After the opera, which, like the meal, was exquisite, we ambled back to my flat. I again felt overcome with gratitude as I opened my door and Tom and I went inside. The flat wasn't huge by American standards, but by Roman standards it was impressive: the cozy sitting room's picture window overlooked a park, and I had my own efficiency kitchen and a small bedroom. Cathy and Mitch understood that I valued my privacy, as I'm sure they valued theirs. I was just a short walk away from the larger flat they shared with Colin, but I had separation; I had a place of my own in one of the finest cities in the world.

Tom and I stood out on the balcony, drinking a final nightcap. I leaned my head on his shoulder and felt like I was in a dream.

LAURA

What's that line from *Godfather III*? "Just when I thought I was out, they pull me back in."

Even comparing Lillian and James to the mafia makes me feel guilty. Disloyal. Spoiled. Because get this: I told Lillian I was pissed about what she'd pulled with Chris, and she seemed sorry. I didn't use the word "pissed," of course, but I said I wasn't interested in being set up with Chris or anyone else. I felt better for standing my ground, for making my boundaries clear. My mantra is *These are your employers, not your friends—beware of getting too close.* I was careful not to be cold with Lillian, but I realized I had to keep her at arm's length.

It was going pretty well, too. Then last Thursday night, I went over to the house because I was supposed to watch the kids while Lillian and James went out. I was tired. The kids had kind of been monsters, and I'd only had about two hours off before I had to come back. I'd had a Red Bull before coming over, but it hadn't kicked in yet.

When Lillian came downstairs to greet me, she was in sweats.

"Fancy party to go to?" I joked.

"Yes, you might call it that," she smiled. She was holding a garment bag that she handed over to me. "Here," she said. "See if it fits."

I took it, completely confused. Inside was a beautiful red silk gown, in my size. Lillian walked over to the entrance hall closet and pulled out a new box of shoes.

"You can borrow my makeup," she said, "and let's see what we can do about your hair. My curling iron is hot."

"Lillian, what's going on? If Chris is—"

"God no!" she said. "I got the message. No, James and I just wanted to treat you to a night out, to thank you for being such an important part of our family."

"Oh wow!" I said, ignoring the "part of our family" bit. "That's amazing, Lillian. You didn't have to do this—I'm more than happy to—"

"Shh—stop blabbing and let's get you ready! The car will be here in twenty minutes."

"But where am I going?"

Lillian was so excited she looked like a kid on Christmas morning. Moments like these, I couldn't help but love her. She was so enthusiastic, so generous. I felt genuine affection for her, and then my boundaries were obliterated.

"To the premiere of the new Marvel movie!" she shrieked, and I shrieked with her. Hugh Jackman? Would Hugh Jackman be there? Please, God, let Hugh Jackman be there.

"*And*," she added, "Sam's going with you. The car's picking him up first!"

Ah, well, that would be great. Sam was one of my best friends and the perfect person to share a premiere with. Lillian didn't know that he wasn't my boyfriend, and that he himself had a boyfriend. I felt a little guilty for the lie. But then again, I hadn't technically told her Sam was my boyfriend, Chris had. I just hadn't bothered to correct her impression. Of course, I was in trouble if they actually met him. Since James was a designer and Lillian a former makeup artist, they had great gaydar.

I gave her a hug, and she took my hand and pulled me up the stairs. Kylie was already in her mother's dressing area, and stood there with an apron tied around her waist. She might have just been six, and was playing with Play-Doh just moments before, but now she was all business about dressing me up.

"Put the dress on first," she instructed. "You don't want to get makeup on it, or to mess up your hair."

The dress . . . oh wow, the dress. How to describe the dress?

"Is this one of James's designs?" I asked.

"Mm hmm," Lillian said. "He's desperate to be home by the time you leave, so he can see it."

The man was brilliant. You know how when something is really well made, you can just tell from the moment you touch the fabric? It was simple, elegant, classy, and sexy all at the same time. And it fit me perfectly. Had Lillian secretly taken my exact measurements or something? The shoes were just as amazing—leather lined on the inside, satin on the outside, with the most beautiful ornate beaded embellishment at the toe. They were like fairy shoes. How could something so high be so comfortable? But they were. The whole combination was magic, pure seamstress-cobbler magic.

Kylie went through her mother's clutch purses to find one I could borrow for the night, while Lillian tamed my hair and applied my makeup. Damn, she was good. I could see why she had been at the top of her craft. Here and there, I asked her what she was doing, so that I might attempt to re-create it on my own at home. I knew I'd never be able to.

Without sounding arrogant, I have to say by the time she and James were done with me they had created a freakin' masterpiece. Let's just say that these people knew how to make beauty from raw materials. They were my designer fairy godmother and godfather, and I was their Cinderella, being whisked off to the premiere to meet Hugh Jackman. I was determined that he would certainly be there.

My carriage (in this case a limo) pulled up with Sam inside. Not wanting to give him a chance to get out and say hello, I kissed Kylie and Lillian and said my good-byes. Lillian took my picture to show James (he hadn't made it in time), and we were off.

The premiere, like Cinderella's ball, was extraordinary—everything I imagined it would be. A-listers wandered about looking A-list. Hugh was gracious when Sam and I introduced ourselves. Cameras snapped. Press peered at me, wondering, I'm sure, if I was a new ingenue they couldn't quite place.

I was supposed to be making spaghetti and watching *Teenage Mutant Ninja Turtles* with the kids tonight. But instead I was here. In heaven. Life is funny that way.

Needless to say, when I showed up at work the next day and Lillian suggested we go out for lunch while the kids were at a playdate so that I could tell her everything, I immediately agreed. When she inquired about Sam, I fessed up and told her we were just friends. She didn't press the point, and moved into asking me about my plans for the weekend. She was hungry for connection and she was doing her best; she was reaching out. Was that really so bad?

CHAPTER FIVE

· ·

Boundaries

Saying "Yes" and Meaning "No, Hell No, Absolutely No!"

The subject of boundaries fascinates us. Boundaries are applicable to all areas of our lives—with our parents, partners, and kids; with our work; and with our friends. If a celebrity nanny knows how to establish and maintain good boundaries, she can teach us a lot. She immediately has our respect. There is nothing—nothing—easy about setting boundaries in the world of Hollywood, so if she's setting them well, she is the one choosing the jobs, rather than the jobs choosing her. Most are not in such a position. Boundaries makes men of boys, women of girls—and super-nannies of well-paid babysitters. Studying the way people maneuver through setting boundaries and keeping them with finesse (or not!), can teach us loads not only about personal and business relationships in the celebrity world, but also about the way human beings operate.

LOADED QUESTIONS

Most nannies will answer the following questions, posed by parents, with resounding affirmation, even if, inside, "yes" is the last answer they want to give.

1. "Do you think I'm doing a good job as a parent?"
2. "I must be the best boss you've ever had, right?"
3. "You would tell me if my wife were having an affair, wouldn't you?"
4. "Did you love your Christmas gift?"
5. "Do you mind working this weekend?"
6. "My secrets are safe with you, right?"
7. "Do you mind cleaning the bathrooms today? The house-keeper is home sick."
8. "I bet we gave you the biggest bonus you've ever had, right?"
9. "Are you okay with using your new car for work?"
10. "You don't mind working New Year's, right?"
11. "Can you work fourteen days straight while we're away?"
12. "Do you mind not talking to me directly? Anything you need to tell me can go through our personal assistant."

Say you work in the accounting business, or in sales or some such. Your boss wants you to work the weekend. She's asking you to finish a big project, and time is of the essence. There's nothing you'd rather do than switch off and forget about that thing we call work. If you know that a big promotion is on the table, you probably bite the bullet and spend your well-earned weekend nose to the grindstone. Or maybe, instead, you're feeling brave, or you're a bridesmaid in your best friend's wedding, or you're just downright fed up with working weekends, so you refuse. What happens? Perhaps your boss gets cheesed off and, come Monday, you have it out. Or maybe she understands your dilemma and is perfectly sympathetic about it. Your management of the situation will determine the course of your relationship—and career.

Now, imagine your boss isn't just some lady in business pumps and a pencil skirt—she's a celebrity, and the word "no" is a word she rarely hears. People go out of their way to accommodate her in the hopes that she'll toss them one of her famous pouty-lipped smiles or a moment of her time. Every country needs some figurehead to look up to, and in America, it's celebrities instead of a royal family. This is why tabloids sell. You see, your boss isn't just a boss—she's fucking *royalty!*

Celebrity is like a drug. Being worshipped is intoxicating— or so rumor has it—and we are a culture of enablers. Starry-eyed members of the general public pour generous doses of awe and admiration on celebrities. You all know if you bumped into Kim Kardashian at Starbucks, you would tell your friends. You might even whip out your iPhone, snap a pic, and within minutes your Facebook page would read "Besties!—with KK at Starbucks." Celebrities, in turn, reward those who give them recognition. In the case of the random meeting at Starbucks, they offer a smile, a picture, perhaps an autograph. In the case of the fawning employee, they offer job security. Anyone who doesn't play along gets kicked out of the game. Basically, it's a breeding ground for codependent relationships.

So, if you're a celebrity nanny, the unspoken expectation is that you'll say yes to whatever you're asked to do—if you're even asked. Many celebrities, or the staff they surround themselves with, will just tell you what to do. No isn't an option, so why even pretend it is?

All celebrity-staff relationships are marked by this dynamic, but the nanny's relationship with her employer is especially complicated. You are the one taking care of their children. You possibly live on-site, and you see the most intimate makeup-less moments of someone who is accustomed to the spotlight. So when you're asked to work the weekend, even if you were supposed to have it off, guess what? You're working the weekend. You're paid excellent money—far more than you would get working for a "regular" family. Far more than you would get working retail, and far more than you would get as a clerk in a law firm. By taking that money and being allowed into the inner sanctum, you have made a pact.

And that pact means that though you haven't sold your soul, you have sold the control of your daily life.

Parents sometimes choose a nanny who doesn't display a strong penchant for boundaries, or who is a little insecure and a people pleaser. They think those nannies will work harder and longer hours because they're so desperate to be near the celebrity life. We've seen many clients who will refuse to hire a prospective nanny who asks about her time off. In their minds, she's the type who will fly the coop if she's treated like a dog. But how, you ask, can the parents tell what nanny's made of from the outset? How do playground bullies figure out who the most vulnerable victims are? It's like they have some sort of radar for it.

Nanny Cindy was available and on call day and night. But during one dreary winter week, her charges brought home the flu and she was unlucky enough to catch it. The kids recovered lickety-split, but, a few days later, Cindy was still at home sick. When the parents called to see if she could pick up the kids from school, she informed them that going more than ten feet from the loo was asking for trouble. They persisted, she refused, and she lost her job for it.

Sometimes, the boundary issues that come up aren't about hours at all. They may be about setting a clear division between the nanny's work and her personal life. (Laura's frustration with her boss for setting her up on a date—pages 80–83—is a good example of this.) Many nannies we know have firm rules about not letting their personal lives cross over to work. For some reason, this seems to be easier for mannies, but more about that in a bit! It's normal—even *civil*—that mums and dads will ask questions about the nanny's life. But because the nanny is in the center of the family's life, she must be careful about how much she shares.

There are good reasons why, when asked about your weekend plans, it's better to say, "Oh, I'm not sure yet," than to say, "I'm going to so-and-so musical with my new boyfriend." With the first response, the boss might shrug and think, *Poor old bird doesn't have much of a life, does she?* With the second response, the boss might think either of the following: *I hear tickets to that musical are expensive! I'm paying her too much! Or, Why didn't I know about this boyfriend? What if she's hiding something? What if it's serious and she's thinking of getting married and having babies and leaving? Oh my gosh, I think I'd better call Julie at the agency.*

One nanny, Margie, became far too close to her boss. Margie was happy to listen to the mum's problems—she wanted to be helpful. Plus, the mum was the only human being over three years old with whom she worked, and it was nice to have adult company on occasion. But after a time, the mum began to rely on her for emotional support; Margie was more like a husband or best friend than a paid employee. She began to feel responsible for not only the kids' happiness, but also the mum's well-being. Keep in mind that Margie was half the age of the mum, and this was her first big job.

Then Margie started volunteering as a tutor to underprivileged youth in her free time, and her boss found out about it.

"I saw your Instagram picture of that darling little girl," the mum began. "Who is she?" (First off, bad idea to have your boss able to see your Instagram feed, Margie. Rookie mistake.)

Margie told her about the program, and the mum said, "That's so great! Do you really think that's a good idea, though? I mean, my kids just need you so much—if you have more hours available, I'd love to have you here at the house." Realizing she was edging into hot water, Margie soothed the mum's worries and ego by downplaying her volunteer activities, and never, ever, let the mum find out about them again.

In reality, however, there are some nannies who *want* the boundaries to disappear. They want to blend in with the family as much as possible, and they forget that there's a division at all. It's understandable: the families can be fabulous—fabulously wealthy, fabulously beautiful, fabulously alluring. Nannies want to be woven into the fabric of the family's life; they believe they're indispensable. Silly nannies. Kids grow up—there is a very natural expiration date for the job. Also, look at the very nature of the disposability of marriages in Hollywood! And these are the people they've sworn to love "till death do us part," not just someone they signed a nanny contract with.

TOP SIX BOUNDARY BENDERS *EVER*

For nannies:

6. Accompanying dad to a red carpet event while mum is out of town.

5. Attending child's parent-teacher conference without telling mum and dad it was coming up.

4. Talking to the child about the Lord Jesus, even though mum and dad are Jewish.

3. Tying a charge's head in red yarn to cure his ear infection. (Nanny was very superstitious and swore it worked.)

2. Putting the kid in your own gym's childcare while you work out.

1. Sleeping with dad, mum, or, as we mentioned in the case of Mary (page 66), both at once!

For mums and dads:

6. Mandating what soap, shampoo, conditioner, and body lotion nanny must use, and what detergent she must use to wash her clothes. (Control freak, anyone?)

5. Introducing nanny as "my daughter," "my sister," or "my wife."

4. Sleeping with nanny or the nanny's husband or wife.

3. Telling the nanny that if she can't stay abroad with you longer than you'd originally told her, she'll have to pay her own airfare home (pages 33–34).

2. Pulling a guilt trip on the nanny to extend her hours, telling her they're working late when they're really out to dinner.

1. Hiding a camera in nanny's room that watches her while she sleeps.

Julie spends a lot of time with her nannies, talking them down from this, that, or the other boundary violation. But even she is not available all the time. She tells everyone—everyone—that she is unavailable after six o'clock. "Sure, you can call, but I'm not going to pick up. Please leave a message at the tone."

This has been hard for some, particularly for clients who presume they are above the rules. And why wouldn't they make this assumption? Everybody in their life, from their cook to their attorney, drops everything for them at the drop of a hat. Yes, Julie's unavailability is met with a puzzled response, but she doesn't waver. Every time she says no, she's also saying, *My personal life is valuable.*

Julie sets boundaries not only with her time, but also with her willingness to put up with bullshit. She calls it like she sees it, whether the person sitting in her office is Scary Spice or John Denver ("Both of whom did sit in my office, by the way, and both of whom had to tell me explicitly who they were and what they did. Embarrassing stories on my part, to be told at another time!"). One sixty-five-year-old film executive she worked with called to complain about the amount of money he was spending on baby nurses. His wife wanted a slew of them, at forty-five dollars per hour. "Who would have thought a harmless flirtation could lead to this sort of expense!" he groaned.

"Babies don't arrive from nowhere," Julie countered. "So here we are with the result, and it's no use grumbling over it."

"Nobody talks to me that way," he said after a pause. She waited for him to hang up on her, but he didn't. In fact, Julie has come to believe that when she draws a line in the sand, and tells her clients that if it doesn't work for them, she totally understands, it actually makes them feel *safe*. They know she's not trying to take something from them because of who they are. And if a nanny adopts the same sort of attitude, and moves through her life with the same kind of respect, love, *and* distance, she'll be treated like (and given) gold.

Stella has had confrontations regarding her boundaries similar to what our nannies have experienced. Once when she was working as a baby nurse, her husband had quite a severe asthma attack and had to go to urgent care. Needless to say, Stella was worried about him. The mum and grandmum were out shopping, and when they returned, she told them what happened and that she needed to go check on her husband. They complained to the agency afterward that she was unprofessional. She quit immediately. Perhaps some would say she overreacted. But she had drawn her line in the sand, and they crossed it.

Saying no is an art form. Barnes & Noble has hundreds of books in its self-help section on how to say this two-letter word, and yet most people are far from mastering it. We believe "no" is a muscle which needs to be exercised more. Not every nanny is ready. When the nanny has grown overly accustomed to a certain lifestyle, or is too attached to the rich and famous, saying no will feel way too scary to contemplate.

Just as with all of us, when it comes to boundaries, the best thing nanny can do is acknowledge that she is making a choice. Let's go back to how we began this chapter, with that request for you to work on the weekend. If you say yes because you are angling for a promotion, you must own that. You have made a deal with yourself. The nanny who bails on throwing her best friend's baby shower is likewise making a choice. The nanny who stays in a job even though a better life might be waiting for her if she takes a risk is also making a choice. However blurry boundaries seem, the worst thing you can do is shrug and say there's nothing you can do, it's out of your hands. Because then you are still making a choice—to be a victim.

Nanny vs. Manny

For better or worse, we have a ringside seat to the sociopolitical climate of child rearing and the service industry. Thus we have plenty of observations and opinions about how women, in particular, are trained to operate and what kind of people work as nannies. People who become nannies tend to be caretakers, for obvious reasons. They put the needs of others before their own, compromise their own interests to keep things running smoothly, smile and nod when what they'd really like to do is give someone a good and well-deserved smack upside the head. Combine this predisposition toward caregiving with the youth of most nannies, add in a large dollop of high salary and slather it all with celebrity worship, and you're bound to get a perfect recipe for all kinds of boundary issues.

As much as we hate to say it, there is a definite gender dynamic at work in the nanny arena. As a warning, this paragraph includes a lot of stereotypes and generalizations . . . all which happen to be true. You are probably familiar with the statistics about how men make more than women. But studies show that that's largely because men *ask* for more money. They are less likely to put up with being treated poorly. They are less likely to be strong-armed into chairing the elementary school's auction committee when they really don't have time for it. They are less likely to trade a romantic date for work. They are more likely to claim and take time off for themselves. And when it comes to our field, mannies are absolutely better about setting boundaries than nannies.

Here's the part that really sucks, though: employers are better at *respecting* it when men set boundaries. We could write a whole dissertation about this subject, but it's probably preferable for everyone if we stick to writing this book.

Pure and simple, there is a double standard when it comes to male and female nannies. Men can say no without fear; women can't. So what's the answer? Hell if we know! But we do know this needs to be changed, one employer at a time, one woman at a time. We're not expecting you to burn your bra or anything (going braless is, of course, a nanny no-no), but come on, ladies, stand up for yourselves!

KIRSTEN

Oui, *oui* seems to be all I'm capable of saying. Only not to the people who matter most. I feel like such a jerk. Or, as the French would say, *le con.*

Oui, we are here in France—Ron, Tess, the kids, and I— because Ron's filming a new movie. The hotel in Paris is gorgeous, the dining is amazing, and the kids and I have seen everything on my list twice. Derek and Ali have been great sports about tromping around Paris with me. When they whine about being tired, we just stop for hot chocolate and a *pain au chocolat* and all's good in the world again. Then it's onward to the Louvre, a boat trip on the Seine, the Moulin

Rouge. (Okay, not there. I did that on my day off, much to Derek's disappointment.)

But days off are few and far between. I've been on the clock day and night six days a week, with only one day off to go out on my own and do everything a cute American twentysomething with cash in her pocket can do. Which, as it turns out, is quite a lot, thanks to the amazing shopping on Faubourg Saint-Honoré.

Then yesterday, on what was supposed to be our last day, I started packing up the kids' stuff. Tess came in and said, "Oh Kirsten! I forgot to tell you—we're going to need to stay a bit longer."

"Oh?" I asked. "How much longer?"

"Another week, maybe two."

I frowned. I loved Paris, but I had a serious conflict. Surprisingly (for she's not always all that observant), Tess noticed my distress.

"What is it?" she asked.

"My best friend, Gina—I'm hosting her baby shower on Sunday. Remember, I let you and Ron know last month," I said, attempting to keep the panic out of my voice. "I did as my work agreement says and wrote a request for time off thirty days in advance, and got it approved through the business office. Sasha put it on the schedule."

"Oh, the schedule, you know it's always changing; this sort of thing happens all the time with us. It's part of your job, Kirsten, to be available when we need you." Tess said, frowning. "Just ask her to move the shower by a couple of weeks."

No, I thought, *this sort of thing does not happen all the time. Most people I know do not change their international travel plans at the last minute.*

"I can't," I said. My voice was tight as I swallowed back tears. "Gina's due in just a couple of weeks. If I stay, I might miss the birth, too—"

"Oh," Tess said. "Are you her birth partner or something?"

"No, nothing like that, but I do want to be at the hospital."

"Well," Tess said, "I suppose all we can do is hope she's late. First babies usually are!" She laughed her silvery little laugh and walked off.

What could I do? She hadn't really given me a choice. And even if she had, I'm not sure what I would have done. I knew I needed to keep Tess and Ron happy and prove how essential I was to the family. I didn't want some other help person swooping in and taking my place.

A few hours later, after much hand-wringing, I called Gina. I expected some crackling static on the line, like long-distance calls in old-timey movies. But the connection was crystal clear.

"Hi, Gina," I said.

"Hey, Kirsten! I was just thinking about you. I swear I'm about to freaking pop. I feel like a watermelon."

"Yikes," I said, looking down at my flattish, baby-less belly.

"You calling from France? How is it?"

"Well," I replied timidly, "I was just calling to talk to you about that. See, um . . . Tess extended our trip. We're staying a few more weeks."

Silence on the line. Then, "The baby shower's Sunday."

"I know it is. I told her. But they really need me."

"They really need you? Uh, I need you, you dummy! I'm having a baby, remember? I'm big and gassy and grumpy! You were going to have the shower at your new apartment. Remember that?"

"Yes, of course I do. And I've got it all figured out—Annie's got the keys to my place, and she's going to take over as hostess. Then I'm taking you for a spa day, just us, when I get home."

Another silence on the line, thicker than the most deca-dent French dessert.

"Kirsten. Please. If you're not back for a few weeks, you might miss the birth, too."

"First babies are usually late," I said.

"Oh, well, that's great news."

"I'm sorry, Gina. I really am, but I have to go."

"Kirsten, hold on. Please, just think about it. You have to work, I get that. But you have to say no to these people once in a while. It's just a job, after all. I mean, if you can't say no to them now, for this, then when will you?"

I paused. I knew she was right. But a part of me, a part that seemed to be growing stronger than other parts—namely loyalty, generosity, considerateness—had already taken hold.

"Shoot, listen, Gina, you're starting to break up. I've got to go. I'm really sorry. What? . . . I can't hear you . . . Shoot, I'm sorry, Gina. Okay, talk to you soon. Bye."

I hung up, adding that little "bad connection" lie to my already mounting guilt. God, I was becoming such an asshole. Now I wasn't sure what kind of welcome I'd receive when I got home. Maybe no welcome at all, and maybe no friendship, either.

JEREMY

At my first meeting with Mr. Black's house manager, I'd said, "Money's not my thing. No disrespect, but I'm not going to work on my days off no matter how much extra you pay me, and it's probably good if we're all clear on that."

When I later relayed the conversation to Carly, the other nanny, she told me I was full of shit.

"You did NOT say that to him."

"I did," I protested, "and you should, too. Come on, Carly, you're exhausted. Chase doesn't need someone holding his hand every single second—you should be able to take a weekend off."

"You're right," she said, rubbing her eyes. "Ugh, my list of grievances is getting crazy long. Between my hours and the maid duty, you know."

"What maid duty?"

"What do you mean, what maid duty? Since Mrs. Black left with two housekeepers two weeks ago, we've been filling in. Come on, Jeremy—you've been doing it, too, right?"

I had no idea what she was talking about, and told her so. No one had asked me to mop, vacuum, or dust.

Now Carly looked like she was on the verge of tears. "Seriously?" she asked. "You mean to tell me that I've been busting my butt to be a good team player in crisis, and no one's even *asked* you to pitch in?"

Part of me wanted to tease Carly about her use of the word "crisis" to describe being down to only one full-time housekeeper, but I didn't want her tears on my conscience, so I refrained.

"Look, don't get mad. You've got to just set up a meeting with Big Boy," I said, referring to our nickname for the house manager. "Lay it out for him calmly. Explain that you need your time off, and that you can't fill in for the housekeepers anymore. You can even use me, if you want—tell him that we talked and you want to be treated the same way I am, that it's only fair."

"Okay, so clarify this for me," she said. "Big Boy never asks you to work extra hours?"

"No, he still asks," I said, "but I refuse. And every time, there's a little hitch in our giddyup for a few days. But it never turns into something big, and a few days later he asks again and we have the joy of repeating the whole process. Unless, of course, there is a major crisis; then I'll go into work."

"Okay," she said, looking at me bravely. "I'll do it!" Not at that moment, of course, given we were having this conversation naked, in her bed. (Have I not mentioned this awesome perk of working with all women? The bonus: since Carly and I usually just passed each other on our shifts, it wouldn't get awkward if we stopped seeing each other.)

I thought I'd been a great coach to her. But great coaching, it turns out, isn't enough. A few days later, she caught me by the arm on my way out.

"How'd it go with Big Boy?" I asked her.

She narrowed her eyes; she was seething. "Oh, just great," she said. "I said exactly what you told me to say, and he said, 'Carly, those are the rules for Jeremy. These are the rules for you. So take it or leave it.'"

Well, crap. That sucked, but I didn't see how it was my fault.

"Huh," I said, and frantically searched for something helpful to say, something that would explain away what was pretty clearly a double standard. "Maybe it's because I laid it out in the beginning? You know, before I was hired."

Her answer was to flip me off. Looks like our roles were pretty clear: I was the bad guy who had time off and she was

the martyr who took one for the team. And we would no longer be sleeping together—that much was also pretty clear.

TRACY

Well, our Roman holiday came to an end. We were
heading back to the States, and my time feeling like
the umbrella-twirling star of a classic romantic comedy was
about to expire. No longer would I look in the mirror and
imagine I saw an Audrey Hepburn–style funny face (that's
so gorgeous there's nothing funny about it) but a real, funny
British nanny–style face. Ah, the real world.

Tom and I met at the café where we'd run into each other
the first time. The Italian summer sun shone down on the
rows of tables, reflecting off the set silverware and glasses.
Tom was already at a table, one long, bony leg crossed over
the other, foot a-jangling. When he saw me, he smiled, and
I felt a wave of nostalgia for the passing of this moment that
hadn't even happened yet. It'd been so long since I'd fallen in
love, and just as long since I'd had to say good-bye.

"Hi, Tom," I said with apprehension.

"Hullo, Tracy," he said and smiled that beautiful blue-
eyed smile.

We spent the next few hours sitting there, sipping cap-
puccinos and avoiding what we both knew was coming.
Finally, I checked my phone and saw that it was time to head
back to pack Colin's suitcases. I frowned, feeling that familiar

crease of worry appear between my eyebrows. It had been months since I'd last felt it.

"I need to be off," I said, picking up my bag.

"I know," Tom said. "Can I walk you back?"

We stood up and made our way out to the sidewalk. He took my hand. We walked in silence for a bit while I worked up the nerve to say something.

"Tom."

"Yes?"

"I like you."

"And I like you."

"I wish—"

"Come back and visit me."

"Okay," I said.

He drew me to him, my hands in his, and he rested his forehead with his floppy hair against my forehead. He looked into my eyes.

.   .   .

Three months passed. I settled back into my usual routine: taking care of Colin, taking care of Colin, drinking tea, taking care of Colin. For once I had followed through with a plan to do something for myself and already had a trip back to Rome on the calendar. Tom and I had been e-mailing and Skyping a lot. Mitch and Cathy gave me an entire week off for my trip, which I'd promised to make up for by working over both Thanksgiving and Christmas.

My hands shook as I packed my suitcase. It had been a long, long time since I'd gone on a vacation—a real vacation with no kids in tow, no crying babies, no frazzled mums to manage. I wasn't quite sure what I was going to do with myself, and I didn't know what it would be like with Tom. But I was hopeful, nervous, and excited.

It was everything I hoped it would be, and more. We rode bikes in the Tuscan countryside. We strolled. We cooked elaborate meals together, and had his friends over. We shopped for antiques. We talked about the future. It's strange to say since I work in a domestic service, but it was the most domesticated I'd felt in my life.

On the last night together, we returned to our little café for dessert. The chocolate torte was delicious, and the glass of Moscato d'Asti matched it perfectly. Between bites we held hands across the table. I'm sure our waiter was rolling his eyes in the kitchen, thinking the Italian version of *What a couple of old frumps.* But, I'd have told him, love isn't just for the young and sexy and glamorous.

Out of the blue, Tom said, "Stay."

We sat in silence for a moment, looking down at our intertwined hands.

"I can't," I said. "My job."

"That's too easy of an answer," he said. "I want you to really think about it."

I did. I was in my mid-forties, and this was the first time I'd met someone who I felt was a perfect match for me. What were the chances it would happen again? I was past my peak childbearing years—in fact, having children of my own had been off my radar for years. Tom said he didn't want children, never really felt the desire. He thought we could make a great life together and I believed him and agreed with him.

Maybe I could leave my job after all. Choose a life of my own. I could seize my chance to do something different, to be someone different. I would be an Italian housewife, cooking risotto and gnocchi for Tom while he was at work. I would write novels, or perhaps work at an Italian day care, and then in the evenings Tom and I would be together. We would read out loud to one another, we would visit our families in England twice a year. We would travel together, where *we* wanted to go. On our own terms.

"Stay," he said again. "Think about it."

I didn't sleep at all that night. My flight was to depart at noon the next day. We'd have to leave for the airport at nine, if I decided to go.

Of course I'd go—I took too much pride in my work to just leave my employers in the lurch, especially after they'd been so kind to me. But once I got to California, what then? Would I give notice? Would I return to Italy?

"I do have to go," I told Tom when the alarm rang in the morning. "At least for now. But I'll talk to Mitch and Cathy. I want to come back. I do."

.   .   .

As soon as I got back to the California house, Colin ran to me in his exuberant toddler way. He threw his pudgy hands around my neck. "Tacy ba, Tacy ba!" which I understood to mean "Tracy's back." I took in the smell of him, the feel of his soft little body clutching me. I'd missed him. I was excited to watch this little boy grow up.

As soon as I had the thought, I caught myself. *This is not your child, Tracy.* I knew that. But I've been in this business a long time, and I knew that this family would not dismiss me. If I left before he was grown, it would be my choice, not theirs.

Cathy and Mitch had been kind enough to order takeout from my favorite restaurant, and we all sat around and ate together and talked about my trip. I got the sense they were attempting to get a feel for how serious my relationship might be and how close they needed to be to pulling the trigger and calling the agency.

"Next stop, Rio de Janeiro," Cathy laughed. "I know, you've just gotten back and now it's time to pack again. We leave in two days; can you believe it?"

I needed to think. I needed to talk to them. I needed to talk to Tom. But I knew, from the most inner part of me, that I was going south to Rio, not east to Rome. At least for now.

LAURA

Just because I knew it was coming didn't make it any easier. So when the phone rang early on a Thursday morning and I saw that it was my mom calling, the drop in my stomach was like tipping over the hill of a roller coaster—seeing the sharp slope that's coming and not being able to do a thing to slow the momentum.

My mom broke the news: my grandpa had passed away during the night. Gramps had been sick for a while, and the last time I was home for a visit I had a chance to say the things you say to someone you love if you're not sure you'll ever see him again. It wasn't a shock, but still I was not ready. I knew I was lucky; this was the first time someone close to me had died.

After I'd had some time to calm down, I texted Lillian and told her I was on my way and that I needed to talk to her. I drove over to Lillian and James's, and when I got there, she was waiting.

"Hey, Laura," she said. "What's up? You okay?"

I could feel a lump in my throat. I attempted to swallow. "My mom called this morning. My grandfather died."

"Oh, Laura! I'm so sorry. I know how close you were. That is just terrible."

"Yes," I said, again swallowing. I wasn't going to let myself cry in front of my boss. "The funeral is this weekend. I'd like to go home and see my family."

Lillian looked at me. I couldn't tell what she was thinking, but I could see a slight frown. After a pause, she said, "Hmm. You're on the schedule this weekend, right?"

"I am, Lillian, but I would really, really appreciate it if I could have some time off."

"This is kind of short notice. Kylie has a basketball game on Sunday, and I have a hair appointment that I made months ago. I just don't know, Laura."

Really? You have got to be freaking kidding me.

I could feel the blood rushing to my cheeks. *Oh shit, I'm going to cry.* One tear trickled down my cheek, and then a bunch more. This was not a graceful, elegant cry; this was a full-out bawl.

For a moment, Lillian's face had an expression of surprise mixed with horror. But then I felt her hand on my back, rubbing gently like you would a kid who scuffed his knee.

"Shoot, Laura, I'm sorry. We'll figure it out. You go ahead and go home."

.   .   .

It was how you'd expect it to be—family being family. There was a lot of crying and laughing, eating and drinking too much, and standing around with people you think are related to you but can't quite remember how. The funeral was beautiful and sad, the weather cold and wet.

Early the next morning, my phone buzzed. And buzzed, and buzzed. At first I ignored it, not even bothering to check the messages. But at a certain point I couldn't stand it anymore.

Lillian: "hi laura. hope youre doing ok. hey do you know where kylie's basketball shoes are?"

Lillian: "hey girl. hope everythings alright. found her shoes. but now cant find her uniform. you know where it is?"

Lillian: "still havent heard back. found it. k i'll quit bugging you."

Lillian: "hey laura. i just saw the funniest thing. where are you? text me back."

And on and on and on. I started worrying that she was going to be mad if I didn't respond, so, avoiding my mom's stink-eye, I snuck off to answer the texts as they hit my phone. "Where'd Laura get to?" I'd hear someone ask, as I sat in the bathroom instructing Lillian about whether Caleb liked garlic and giving her my opinion on which dress she should buy. The texts kept coming, and they didn't freaking stop until I got on the plane.

When my mom dropped me off at the airport, she killed the car engine and turned in her seat to look at me. "Laura," she said, "you know this isn't normal, right? This thing with your boss?"

My mom knows me better than anyone, so there was no use denying to her what I'd started to see very clearly for myself. "Yeah, I know."

I was wrecked when I got back to LA, and, to say the least, pissed. Lillian had pestered me all weekend, texting me almost nonstop about shit I'm sure any relatively competent adult could have handled. I was starting to think that maybe Lillian needed more help than I could give her.

On the drive back to work the next day, I noticed my white-knuckled grip on the steering wheel and took some deep breaths to calm down. She'd already texted me four times that morning, and Facebook messaged me once. I felt violated and angry. Like, hello, my grandpa just died? Cut a girl some slack.

I needed this job, but I needed my sanity more. This was getting damned close to being the last straw.

CHAPTER SIX

· ·

The Breakup

On Graceful Departures and Nasty See Yas!

When a nanny leaves a family—regardless of who leaves whom—it can be a messy affair. In other jobs, people generally leave without consequence. "Not a good fit," "leaving to pursue other endeavors," "found a great opportunity elsewhere": these send-offs are so familiar to the rest of the professional world they might as well be scripted. On the employee's last day there may even be parting cupcakes or an office-signed "cheerio" card. With the nanny relationship, parting words may a) not happen at all; b) involve tears, harsh words, and hurt feelings; or c) be wound around a bald-faced lie. (The nanny knows the family is not moving to Mexico. She knows the new woman hanging around the kids all the time is not, in fact, a long-lost relative. She knows the mum's not really planning to quit work to stay at home.) In short, the breakup is rarely a grace-filled process.

A nanny departure can more easily be compared to a romantic breakup. With romances, both parties start out wearing rose-colored glasses. Of course, at the back of your mind, you know it might not work out, but you are choosing to focus on the possibility that it will, that you have found your forever love. This new person is fantastic in every way, and although to some his habits or poor manners might be considered annoying, you consider them cute quirks. He eats with his elbows on the table. He doesn't pay attention when you're talking. He's always checking his phone. And he's always running late. Well, you could use a little lesson in slowing down yourself. But time marches on, and although you have a nagging feeling that he's not right for you, you ignore your gut because there's enough that's good. The sex, perhaps, or the security, the companionship, or your fear that you won't find someone better. Little by little, you grow apart. Then there comes a point where if you have to pick up after him one more time, you're going to blow a gasket. By the time you finally leave, neither of you can remember what you loved about the person, and all you want is to get the hell out.

The exact same scenario applies to nannies. Most nannies, before they either resign or are dismissed, already have that nagging feeling. Sometimes that nagging feeling is the awareness that their employers are having doubts about *them*.

Something is not right. But they stay. Most often they stay because they are attached to the kids. Sometimes they stay because the parents have begged them to. Or they stay because they are convinced that the whole family would collapse if they were to leave. Or they stay because of the money. Or they stay because there's an exciting trip to Europe coming up. Or they stay because they don't know who they'd be without their job. Or they stay because it's right before the holidays and their Christmas bonus and lavish presents are just around the corner. It feels more personal than the office job where someone else will take over and hang up photos of his family vacation in what was once your cubicle, because it *is* more personal. Nannies don't work in a cubicle. They're not shuffling papers. This is a home, where they are immersed in family life. The problem is, it's not their family.

Listen to your gut. Getting attached to the kids is always a part of the job, but a nanny is not a parent, and she must look out for herself. If the nanny tries to quit but is begged to stay, she must consider whether her employer would keep her if she were to beg to keep her job. One cautionary tale we tell our nannies is of the nanny who gave notice because she'd been offered a better, higher-paying job. But the mum pleaded with her not to go—saying what a crucial part she played in their lives. So the nanny stayed, and then two weeks later she was dismissed. Another nanny left her position for the very valid reason that she wanted to go back to school. She'd had a fantastic relationship with her employers, but after she left they told everyone they knew about everything the nanny had ever done wrong. They were pissed she was putting her life ahead of theirs. *You can never predict the fragility of a boss's ego.* Is this a Hollywood thing, a money thing, or a consequence of large egos?

SIGNS NANNY IS GOING TO GET SACKED:

- She finds nanny résumés on the fax machine.
- The kids say they've had a new friend over to play with them, and they tell their nanny that their new "friend" looks a bit like her.
- For the first time in years—maybe ever—her boss calls and says the nanny doesn't need to come into work that day.
- She looks at the house line when it's ringing and sees that it's her nanny agency calling her bosses.
- Another nanny agency calls her and tries to recruit her for a job they've just heard about—and it's *her* job.

As much as parents will tell a nanny they are hiring that they want her to be a part of the family, they will dispose of her at the drop of a hat. The reasons for this can vary. Perhaps, in a weak moment, she grumbled to another member of staff, forgetting he was not her friend, and he didn't hesitate to chuck her under the bus to increase his status. Or maybe the children had grown too close to the nanny, and the parents felt threatened. It could be that the nanny witnessed a moment where the mum or dad was particularly vulnerable, and later that parent is embarrassed. It could be that the dad is taking too much notice of the nanny, and the jealous mum suddenly remembers how the nanny accepted a beer on a long-ago trip.

So, what parents are really saying when they tell a nanny they want her to be part of the family is, "We want you to be part of our family until you do something that really upsets us and then you're gone, just like that. You're out of the house with less fanfare than the departure of dear Uncle Henry during one of his lecherous weekend incidents." Suddenly the people to whom you've dedicated the past years of your life find a new family member more to their liking, and it's cheerio to you—*finito*, *sayonara*, *à tout à l'heure*, and at times just a solemn *adieu*.

When it was time for Mary Poppins to leave, she blew away with the wind, but in the real world, nanny is often shot out of a cannon, never to be spoken of again. Whatever the cause for dismissal, it usually happens quite roughly, like a long romantic relationship that ends via text message.

One nanny we know was traveling to meet her employers at their home in the Maldives. She flew without incident from Los Angeles to New Jersey to catch her connecting flight, but while waiting at the Newark airport she learned that she'd been released. She then was compelled to spend several days in snowy New Jersey, paying for her own hotel room while waiting for the air traffic to ease so that she could get a flight home. She spent the time mopping up her tears and her self-esteem while her suitcase arrived in the Maldives without her. Another nanny relocated for her job, lived with the family for six months, and was told on a Thursday that she needed to be out of the house Friday, with no notice and no severance.

ALL IN THE FAMILY

The line that's possibly the most misconstrued in the nanny-parent arena is "We want you to be part of the family." It separates the nanny arena from most other work environments. Think on it: "We want you to be part of our family" is not offered as a carrot when interviewing for any other job.

Most parents say this with the best intentions at heart. To experienced nannies, it's a red flag. "I've turned down jobs because one of the first things the family said at the interview is they would want me to be part of their family," said manny Jerry.

"I don't want to be part of someone's family; I have my own family. I love kids, and I'm a great nanny, but it's a job."

Some naïve nannies will say, "Oh, how sweet!" when the parents express this sentiment. More balanced parents will actually mean "Hey, we're good people and pretty normal by all accounts, so we will be good to work for." They use it as a way to show that they are not as batshit crazy as the people the nanny worked for previously. But never does this sentiment come with a "till death do us part" agreement.

When parents say, "We want you to be part of the family," here is what experienced nannies hear:

- You will always be on call.
- We will always debate your overtime; family works for free.
- You will love us so much, we're hoping you'll forget this is a job.
- Forget your own life; what small piece of life you may have comes second.
- We're your boss, we'll love you until we don't, then we'll find another you to love.
- Never come to us with the word "boundary" in a sentence—that's not what families are about.
- We will guilt you into getting whatever we want.
- Yes, we are screaming, ranting, name-calling loonies, but, at the end of the day, this is family!

The nanny hadn't done anything wrong, by the way—the mum just decided it wasn't working out. When Julie reminded the mum that, given the short notice of the dismissal and the fact that the nanny would have to pay for a hotel room, severance would be a reasonable proposition, the mum said, "Are you suggesting that I'm a bad person?" To which Julie replied, "That's not for me to say!"

Following are a few other instances of nannies dismissed in an abrupt way, to put it politely.

Nanny Jane was escorted off the property of her live-in position, without her possessions, by armed security after a celebrity mum believed that Jane had stolen a diamond watch. Mum later found the watch. She'd popped it in the safe . . . for—yes, you guessed it—safekeeping! And no, she didn't apologize for her error.

Nanny Gretchen was thrown out of the family's Mercedes, on Sunset Boulevard, miles from a bus stop and without her purse or wallet, because when she was cleaning up the child's room she put Barbie's pink plastic spoon in the fork drawer of Barbie's house!

Nanny Joanne was fired because she refused to take a crying baby out of the car seat whilst the mother was driving ten miles over the speed limit on Pacific Coast Highway because she was late for an audition. Sure, let's maim the child, but definitely do not be late for a part.

Typically nannies are not given a single day to absorb that they will no longer be hanging out on a private beach, eating caviar, or jet-setting around the world as "part of the family." They are not given a letter of recommendation because of liability issues. All they are permitted to use as reference is the business manager, who will answer only as to whether or not she was employed and for what period of time—that's it. And no matter how integral they've been to the family's life, they are often not given the chance to say good-bye to the kids. Most painfully for many, they are told they must destroy all photographs of themselves with the children.

These nannies have given and sacrificed, and they are left with nothing. Sometimes—and let us be clear that this is their own bloody fault—they have absolutely no money saved. This is *most* annoying. We just don't get it. If a nanny is making a healthy salary and not covering any of her expenses, why doesn't she save? It's all about self-care, really, and playing a game of defense. With high-profile jobs like these, a nanny must always be on her toes. She must always anticipate that it could all go away with a snap of some well-manicured fingers. From day one of a new job, she must be readying herself for her exit. She must never forget that she's nothing other than an employee, and no matter how much good she does, she will be considered a bad one when the employers are looking to sack her.

NANNIES BEHAVING BADLY

It's not just the bosses who give harsh good-byes, or leave under less-than-kosher circumstances. The following are our most memorable (by which we mean piss-poor) nanny exits:

1. "I need to leave to take care of my granny." (Never mind that Granny's as fit as a butcher's dog.)

2. "I'm changing my career." (Never mind that at the dinner party last week where she happened to be working, the employer's so-called friend offered her $20,000 more a year to go work for them.)

3. "I was homesick." (Nanny's response after, having lived with the family in Paris for five months, she woke up one morning, left for the airport, and flew home—without telling anyone.)

4. "I'm working the full hours laid out in my contract. I really didn't think I'd be working *all* of them."

5. "The job is much harder than I thought. Children need attention *all the time!*"

We know the employers sound like the bad guys here. But every dual-dimensional bad guy has a compelling motive. Remember, these parents are positively preyed upon. They are a commodity, and people have tried to make money off of them for the entire span of their celebrity (and some of them have been celebrities since infancy). To convince them that it's not so is like trying to convince a barking Chihuahua that no one is impressed or intimidated. People who have been their friends try to exploit them; people who have been their employees try to blackmail them. It's ugly, and in many ways both they and their nannies are victims of celebrity culture.

What's more, most of them have been guarded from unpleasantness for so long that they have lost their sense of . . . well, manners. As we covered in chapter one, they have someone else tell a nanny they're not hiring her. And if they can have someone else take care of an unpleasant task like firing her, they will delegate. If they are displeased with an element of their nanny's performance, instead of managing it the hard way by talking to her about it (which might be unpleasant or make her mad at them), they have their house manager simply replace her. And it's not that they don't feel guilty about this. They do. But to counter that guilt, they justify their decision by villainizing the nanny.

It's a harsh side of human nature, no doubt about it. And all the nanny can do is protect herself.

MATCHES MADE IN HEAVEN

Let's not assume all endings are dire. We wanted to bring you a few stories of nanny unions that thrived, and where balance—be it of love or of an outside interest—proved possible despite demanding jobs. It *does* happen!

Nanny Ellen, originally from Iowa, moved to Los Angeles when she turned twenty-nine, wanting to have a bit of adventure before she turned thirty. She was also keen to be close to the beach. She was hired by an entertainment couple who had two young boys and told Julie that they wanted a nanny over fifty who had raised her own children. Julie persuaded them to meet Ellen and they fell in love with her. Ellen worked for them for four years, which just goes to show that Mary Poppins can show up looking very different from what we think. Then Ellen met a man, got engaged, and planned her wedding all while still managing her full-time traveling position with the family. The parents paid for her honeymoon and the boys were ring bearers at her wedding.

Manny Christopher was born and raised in Los Angeles. He worked as a personal trainer, taught karate at the YMCA, and tutored kids for the SATs. He helped a family who had an eleven-year-old boy and a thirteen-year-old girl with after-school/homework care. He also taught them, and some of the neighborhood kids, martial arts. When the kids no longer needed after-school care, the parents, and the parents of the neighborhood kids, got together and rented a studio space so Christopher could focus on his dream of opening a martial arts center for children.

Nanny Sue, who was thirty-two, moved to Los Angeles from Portland with her husband, who was a sound technician. They'd been married since their second year of college. Sue had worked as a teacher in Oregon but decided to start nannying as there were "fewer politics involved." Ha! Julie wanted to tell her, "This is the city of politics!" but thought better of raining on her Hollywood parade. Sue was hired by a wonderful family, and soon after that became pregnant herself. Though it wasn't planned, she was thrilled nonetheless. The parents didn't mind at all. Sue worked until she was eight months pregnant; then the family used a temp for a few months until Sue went back to work, baby daughter in tow. That was three years ago, and, last we heard, the family and nanny are still together.

The Pros and Cons List

Once, when Stella was planning to leave a job but hadn't told her employers yet, she came across a notebook with a pros and cons list written . . . about *her*. Under "pros" it said things like "great with the kids." Under "cons" it said things like "used to stay late—now is running out the door at five o'clock." Surreal as it was to read such a list about herself, she saw what was happening. Her employers were feeling Stella pulling away. They had a nagging feeling that she was having a nagging feeling. It was time to say their good-byes, before they forgot what they loved about one another in the first place.

It's true that good-byes are rarely handled well, but sometimes they're not terrible, even if not exactly easy. And sometimes the breakup isn't about the family at all, but about another part of her life that just could not work with her job. Breakups are simply a part of life, and, as any single man or woman will tell you, you learn with each one, and they get easier and easier to handle.

And so we end this chapter by asking, whether in love or in Nannywood, is it such a bad thing to enter into a relationship with an exit plan? Does that make you a commitment-phobe, or does it make it more likely that you will be true to yourself? For Nannywood, we think it's the latter. And when you really think about it, can't we all stand to be a bit truer to ourselves? Let's see how our four nannies navigate this tricky part of the nanny relationship.

KIRSTEN

oly, holy fuck! I don't know what happened, I don't have a clue why, but I was fired today. Effective immediately. Actually, faster than immediately, as I never even got in the door this morning.

I was on my way to work when Sasha called my cell. "Hey," she said. "Can you meet me at the storage unit instead of going to the house?" I thought it was strange, but maybe we were getting another fill-a-trash-bag-with-clothing "shopping" spree. Then I thought that Tess and Ron had gotten into some drag-out fight or something, or there was some other drama she wanted to give me a heads-up about. I honestly didn't think *I* was the drama.

I parked and found Sasha sitting on a bench, looking very official with a briefcase of papers in hand. "Kirsten," she said, looking down at her papers, "I'm sorry to inform you that we are no longer in need of your services."

"*What?*" I said.

Sasha cleared her throat. "As is stated in your employment contract, upon release you need to sign the following paperwork. I'll also need you to give me your ID badge and keys, and I'll need to look at your phone and make sure it's clear of proprietary images and information. It shouldn't take too long."

"Sasha," I said, somewhere between hyperventilating and a total tearful breakdown, "can you back up a second? Why are you acting like this? We've become too close for this shit. Tell me what's going on. What did I do wrong? I have no fucking idea where this is coming from."

She softened ever so slightly. Which is to say, barely. "I don't know," she said. "This stuff just happens sometimes." Then she squared her shoulders and got all businesslike again.

My tears fell then, and fast. Professionalism be damned. Hadn't Sasha and I just last week danced around a hotel living room like idiots when we had both been working for hours on end and needed to let off steam? She wasn't even my fucking boss—why was she the one doing this? Why weren't Ron and Tess?

That's how it went for a while. I dug in my purse for tissue and blubbered. I found my key, I gave her my phone, I signed the papers. I hadn't even looked at the paperwork, really, when I was hired. Now I read it through the watery mess that was my vision. "*The Recipient shall hold in perpetuity all Proprietary and Confidential Information in strict confidence, not disclosing any Information in any manner whatsoever. Accordingly, the Recipient acknowledges any use of the Proprietary and Confidential Information by the Recipient would amount to legal conversion, theft, or embezzlement.*" It was a litany of things I couldn't do and couldn't say, backed up by legal threats. I felt like Jason Bourne or something, like the CIA had just erased years of my identity.

"W-w-w . . . what about Derek and Ali?" I asked. "Don't I get to say good-bye to them?"

Sasha sighed then, and when I looked at her, I noticed for the first time how tired she looked. She was pale, with circles under her eyes, and there was a lot more gray in her jet-black hair than I'd ever noticed before. "Technically," she said, "no."

This set off the waterworks again. Not that I'd ever really stopped.

"Listen, Kirsten," she said, "I'll tell you what. Why don't you write each of them a letter saying good-bye? I'll give them to the kids. Tess and Ron will probably read the letters first, so don't say anything you wouldn't want them to see or that would make them keep it from the kids."

"O-o-okay," I whimpered.

We walked back to our cars, and Sasha gave me an encouraging squeeze on the shoulder. "Good luck," she said. No "Hey, let's keep in touch!" No "Don't forget, we're still friends." We weren't, I realized. We probably never had been.

What else, I wondered, had I gotten so wrong?

I drove home and crawled into bed. I'm still here, but at least I'm not in the fetal position anymore.

I keep playing the past few days and weeks through my mind. Was it Ron? He'd let his eyes linger on me for maybe a second too long last week when I said good night to them. Had Tess noticed? Was it Ali? I'd given her a hard time about wanting to wear makeup. Did she tell her parents? Had Derek gotten mad at me for something, and followed through on the threat he made way back when, that he would throw himself against a wall and tell his parents I'd done it? No, he wouldn't have . . . I don't think. Or was it the way I called for the car to come around for all of us the other day, and joked to the driver, "You know how we are in this family—always just a minute late!" I'd noticed Tess raise an eyebrow, and kicked myself for saying it. I had expressed too much familiarity. I'd presumed too much.

My mom—the only person I felt I could call without worrying about the legal ramifications—thinks I'm going to make myself crazy wondering why. The only reason to care about why, she says, is if I think I can prevent making the same mistake in the future. But I'm not sure there's anything to learn from this. She's also worried about my finances. "How much have you saved?" she asked before we hung up.

"Don't worry," I said. In reality, when I find the courage to look at my savings account, it will not be reassuring. It will, in fact, be terrifying. But I'll deal with that tomorrow. And I'll call Julie tomorrow. And I'll write my good-bye letters to the kids tomorrow. Today, I just need to stay here in bed.

JEREMY

Mr. Black freakin' *cried* today. Not that that piece of information will ever go further than this, or I'd get sued before you can say "confidentiality agreement."

I wouldn't share it anyway. It was a really cool moment, so I won't be a douche and make a big deal of it.

I put in my notice a few weeks ago. I've saved enough money to go back to school. Thanks to this job, I'm more sure than ever that I want to work with troubled kids, and I need an advanced degree to do it. I would have quit months ago, but I was pretty worried about Chase. Poor dude's got a lot stacked against him, regardless of how much money he has. Mr. Black had given me pretty much full control over

Chase's life. I picked his therapists, and I talked to his teachers, his coaches, his friends' parents, and the other nannies. We were Team Chase, and I was team captain. Mr. Black was the somewhat distant owner. Mrs. Black was the loving but boozy cheerleader.

Chase needed me, and I wanted to see it through. I felt like I could make a difference in his life. I knew Mr. Black could give me the heave-ho the moment he felt like it—and if he did, so be it—but I wasn't going to be the one to walk away. So I stayed until it seemed like things had stabilized. Chase had weathered the divorce. He was doing okay in school. He had a solid team of people to catch him if he stumbled. And my semester was about to start.

The house manager was cool with my decision, and Mr. Black eventually seemed to understand. But it was harder with Chase.

"Bro," I said when we were shooting hoops one day, "I've got news. I'm going back to school. So I'm not going to be working here anymore."

He had the ball and he stopped short. "So?"

"So nothing," I said. I didn't want to make a big deal out of it. I wanted him to just process it how he needed to. "I'm not going right away—I'll be here a few more weeks. I'm going to help hire someone else. And I'll still come over to hang out sometimes, just not every day."

"I don't need a goddamned babysitter," he said, and his eyes darkened like they do when he's pissed.

"I know you don't," I said.

"Well, then fuck off!" He threw the ball as hard as he could—at my head—and then ran into the house and slammed the door.

I let him go. I knew his deal by now, and I knew he needed to cool off.

When I came over the next day, he didn't want to talk to me at all. So, fine. I pulled out a magazine and read. (Not a terrible way to earn a day's wages.)

Same deal the next day, so I started playing his video games, thinking he would get pissed off at me, or join me. Nada.

Then the next day, I told him I'd be outside playing basketball. He could join me if he wanted. He just grunted. But about twenty minutes later, he came out. I tossed the ball to him, and we started playing H-O-R-S-E. We didn't talk much more until we finished and went in to get some water.

"So when's your last day?" he said.

"The fifth."

"Oh."

"I know you're pissed, Chase."

"I'm not pissed."

"Okay, whatever. But I'm not BS'ing you when I say I'm coming back to hang out with you. And not because you need a babysitter. Because I want to. Cool?"

He shrugged and looked away. I figured that was as good as it was going to get. But I knew Chase, and by now I knew he was going to be okay.

On my last day, Mr. Black was miraculously at home, working. When I went into his office to say good-bye, he asked me to sit down.

"Scotch?" he said. I shook my head. "Oh come on, Jeremy—technically you're not even my employee anymore."

Well, I couldn't be a dick. And it *was* good Scotch. Really good. He poured each of us a glass and he sat down in a leather chair across from mine.

"I know it probably doesn't seem like it," he said, "but I worry about Chase a lot."

Shit, I thought, *is this the guilt trip?* I knew it was coming—*Everyone leaves him, blah blah blah.*

"I also know I've been a pretty crappy dad."

What was I supposed to say to that? Because what I was thinking was, *yep, you have.*

Mr. Black looked at me for a moment, and I willed myself not to say anything. "What I mean to say, Jeremy, is, um, well, thank you. I see my friends in this business; I see their kids in jail, in rehab, in who-knows-what kind of trouble. It's a shit business to raise a family in." To that, I nodded.

"Anyway, I'm pretty sure Chase was headed there, too. But now I think he's going to be okay." This is when I swear to God his eyes filled up with tears and one—a single one— came out. "So, here," he said gruffly, and we clinked glasses. And drank.

TRACY

I counted down the days to Tom's visit. Thirty became ten, became three, became three hours. The world wasn't such a big place! He was coming to Rio on business, and lo and behold we would get an entire weekend together. I'd asked for the time off weeks in advance.

How I'd missed this man! I didn't regret my decision not to quit and move to Rome, though, and Rio was divine. Colin was thriving, such a cheeky and clever little thing. But oh, how I'd missed Tom. I'd even gone so far as to talk to Colin about him. Not that Colin really grasped the significance.

Tom and I had e-mailed, of course, and Skyped and all that, but we'd also written postcards and letters. We talked about how people never corresponded that way anymore, and we'd decided to put pen to paper and to make a permanent record of our courtship. He frequently asked, of course, when I was moving to Rome. I laughed it off, and otherwise evaded the question. I didn't want to be unfair to him, but I also thought his pressure was a wee bit unfair to me. *Why should I leave my job? Why shouldn't he leave his?* Even as I asked myself the question, I knew the answer: Leave his job for what? To move to Hollywood, where I'm only present six weeks out of the year? To globe trot with me around the world, where it would be impossible for him to hold down a steady job, and where he'd most often be alone in a hotel room while I was with Colin?

Tom and I had arranged to meet in his hotel lobby, and I'd worn a new blue dress that I knew he would fancy. The moment he stepped off the elevator, though, I knew. This wasn't a romantic weekend, this was good-bye. His eyes were colder, his posture was stiff. His peck on the cheek was chaste.

I didn't panic, though. In my heart of hearts, I knew this was coming, and I faced it with calm resignation.

"Let's sit, shall we?" I said. I would make this as easy for him as I could.

We talked for a few minutes about his flight, about his work, about Colin. When I couldn't stand it anymore, I blurted, "So this is good-bye, isn't it?"

Tom smiled, took my hands in his. "Tracy," he said, "I really loved you."

Loved? Not love?

"But I think you made your choice. I know you care for me, too, but you'll never be ready to commit to a relationship like this. Not when you've got a more important relationship with your work."

I wanted to argue with him, but I wouldn't. It would be unseemly. It would be tragic, really.

So I nodded and put on a brave face. "You're a good man, Tom," I said. "The best, as a matter of fact." Then I stood and walked out of the hotel. It would be mortifying for him to see me cry.

I wandered around Rio in a bit of a daze. Tom had talked about my "choice," but it didn't feel like I was the engineer of this scenario at all. If I'd had my druthers, we would be sipping cool drinks at the café across the street from his hotel, and then we'd dash back to his room for a proper reunion. I could still do it, I knew. All I had to do was go back to that hotel and tell him that I'd leave my job, I'd move to Rome to be with him. If I did that, it would fix everything. But I wasn't willing to do that. So, this *was* my choice, it seemed. And I had not chosen Tom.

I supposed, in a manner of speaking, it *was* I who had broken up with him.

LAURA

Imagine yourself ten years older than you are now," my mom said. "What would that Laura tell you to do?"

Damn her—I just wanted her to tell me what to do, to give me permission to quit. But being a good mom, she knows better than to put herself in the path of blame or credit for any decision in my life.

That Laura, that ten-years-in-the-future Laura, would look at current Laura in disgust. My nails were bitten down to the quick. My hair was coming out in clumps in the shower— a surefire sign of stress. I was popping a dozen Rolaids a day, and not because I was eating chili nonstop. This job— this "oh-isn't-this-family-so-wonderfully-normal job"—was making me crazy. The hours constantly exceeded what we'd agreed to, my relationship with Lillian had broken every appropriate boundary, and I had forgotten that I ever had a life outside my job.

So why did I stay? The money was part of it. I'd have to get a roommate if I left. My bank statement had seen healthier days, thanks to my binge-shopping habit. Which, ironically, was made worse by stress. I'd have to sell some of my most prized designer clothes. I still needed a job, and one that worked with my school schedule. Better the devil you know than the devil you don't.

The kids were part of it, too. Kylie and I had grown really close, and Caleb was simply one of the coolest kids I'd ever met. I'd miss them so much, and I didn't feel ready to say good-bye. What would happen to all the progress we'd made on the chore chart? They'd deteriorate back into spoiled little monsters, and I wanted better than that for them.

But money wasn't really the reason I stayed, and neither were the kids. It was Lillian. Our relationship, I realized, had become codependent. I resented her for needing me so much, but I also needed her to need me. Or so said my imaginary older self. My current self was still a bit of an idiot about the whole thing.

I did it at the beginning of my workday, but one where I knew Lillian had a packed schedule of her own later so it wouldn't be uncomfortable. We wouldn't have to spend the day hashing it out.

"Lillian," I said, "do you have a minute to talk?" We sat in the kitchen while the kids were cleaning their rooms. (Oh the beautiful chore chart!) "You know I love you guys, but I just can't pursue my studies and have a demanding job at the same time. It's not fair to you, and it's not fair to me. I can stay until the new semester starts in August, if you want me to. And I can help you find someone else."

Lillian frowned. "I wish you would be less black-and-white about this, Laura. You can do both. I've always been supportive about you doing both. And I have to think the money you're making from us will help you finish faster."

"We've tried the route of doing both, Lillian. It doesn't work, and like I said, I want to be fair to you, too, and what you and your family need right now. You need someone who can be more present and available. I'm not that person anymore."

"This is going to be so hard on the kids, Laura," she said. "For their sake, can't we find a way to make it work?"

I knew she'd try this tactic, so I was prepared. "You know I love them, and I plan to be around for them in a different way. I'd love to hang out with them—with all of you guys—when I can."

Lillian rubbed her temples. "I just don't know, Laura. This is putting me in such a terrible position."

Ah, I was ready for this, too. Instead of saying what I wanted to (which was, "It's not really a choice that you have any say about—I'm an at-will employee!"), I actually moved over to her side of the table and put my arm around her. "Remember," I said, "I'm giving you months of advance notice, so I can stay and help you find someone else. And I'd love to, you know, meet for happy hour and stuff when you're able to get away. Maybe we could even finally go shopping together."

She laughed at that. It was something we talked about doing a lot, but we never wanted to bring the kids and it hardly made sense to get a babysitter so that the nanny could take an afternoon and shop with the mom.

Then I pulled out my *coup de grâce*: "You are a fantastic mom, Lillian," I said, and, despite finding some of her practices too lenient, I really meant it. "All those kids really need is you, and they'll be fine."

She squeezed my knee. Then she smiled, and said, "James is going to freak out." But she didn't push it—she got up and left for her day. I knew she'd probably call Julie, and she might complain about me. But I was prepared for that. I would take care to be extra kind and not sour on her, or retort with anything I might regret. She might try to get me back through a higher salary. But I was prepared for that, too, and I knew I wouldn't bite. I didn't want to look back on this moment, ten years from now, and cringe. I wanted to be proud of myself.

When I left for home that evening, I felt completely free. I wasn't, of course—I still had to go back the next day. But I'd effectively said, "Hey, I'm my own woman, and I'm in charge of what's next for me." And I couldn't wait to see what that was.

CHAPTER SEVEN

· ·

The Rebirth

What Nannies Have in Common with Butterflies

W e've now come to the end of our nanny's life cycle—
she's gone, but not forgotten! The life she led with
a particular family has run its natural course, and it's time
to begin anew, either as a nanny for someone else, or doing
something else entirely. The successful nanny—the successful
person, in fact—is one who is able to reinvent herself easily
as she navigates through life. With each incarnation she is
smarter, more nimble and capable, and hopefully a great deal
wiser. On the flip side, those who wallow in self-pity or try
to make their own rules become casualties of the Hollywood
industry. It's not rocket science—there's a way to make a
career as a nanny work, and there's a way to suffer, and the

choice is always within the nanny's control.

This isn't a self-help book; nevertheless, we believe what we've observed, learned, and written about here can help people. Our hope is that *The Nanny Chronicles of Hollywood* will put a smile on the faces of nannies, parents, and all other interested readers alike, as this book was intended to be a gentle poke at Hollywood, which can at times take herself a little too seriously. The role of nanny, however, is a serious and important profession. Through our experiences, we have come to believe that the job of a nanny is a high calling. It is less a job than a vocation.

KIRSTEN

You could say that life has changed for me just a little bit. The view is gone, the salary is gone, the private driver and the travel and everything that came with it is gone. *Poof!*

Here's what I primarily *do* have right now: debt. I was hoping to hold on to my Santa Monica apartment, but am already behind on rent and there's no way I'm going to make it up unless I'm discovered for a big-budget Pantene commercial or something . . . which is unlikely because I look like shit these days.

Here's what else I have: loads of laundry to do. My cash situation was such that I couldn't wait for a job to come through the agency, so I took one on Craigslist to get me through. I make $700 a week, when I used to make $2,000.

They pay me in cash, so that's good, but the job is less than ideal. The job sucks, in fact. If I sound depressed, it's because I am. The family has three crazy kids, which is one thing, but it's the rest of the job that's really doing me in. The parents leave me a list in the morning that includes picking up the house—including the dad's dirty boxers, by the way—doing the laundry, cleaning out the refrigerator, and brushing the dogs. Why did they hire a trained childcare professional if what they really want is a maid?

I was telling Gina all of this, and she made fun of me. Sweet Gina, who did not kick me to the curb when I bailed on throwing her baby shower, who in fact comforted me a ton during those first days after my breakup with Ron and Tess even though she had her own newborn to deal with. "Kirsten," she said, "you didn't used to be such a prima donna. Come back to the rest of us who live down on earth, pretty please. Now hand me those wipes behind you."

Maybe she's right and I need to get over myself a little bit. It's not that I think people who do housework are beneath me, it's just that . . . well, I think I could be channeling my energies toward something better for everyone. But in reality, it might not matter *what* I want. Julie sent me out on a half-dozen interviews, but no job offer. No one even asked me to trial for them.

So I called Julie yesterday, and asked her to give it to me straight. "What's going on?" I said. "What's so wrong with me that no one wants me to trial for them?"

Julie sighed and said, "The people you've been interviewing with have all said the same thing—they don't think you're happy."

"Happy? Well, *of course* I'm not happy! I don't have a real job. I don't have a reference except from stupid Sasha who can hardly reveal anything anyway. How can they expect me to be *happy*?!"

Silence from Julie.

"Julie?"

"Kirsten, why don't you come into the office tomorrow? We'll have a cup of tea and a good cry, and we'll get back on track."

Silence from me, and then, "okay."

So today I went and met with Julie. My shock and dismay about being fired, she said, are written all over my face. I'm carrying so much baggage that people can't even see me behind it. It didn't take much prodding from her for me to start crying. I asked all the dumb questions that had no answers: "Why? What did I do so wrong that they let me go?" I wallowed in my rejection with Julie, and then I promised her I'd find a way to let it all go.

Then I went for a long, long run on the beach. I ran out all of my homesickness for the family I was never actually a part of. I ran out all of the stupid decisions I'd made about money. I ran out all of my wrongheaded feelings about my place in their world.

Tomorrow I'll run again, just to make sure I've got it all out. Then the next day, I have an interview with a really famous single musician. Perhaps one parent will be easier to deal with!

JEREMY

I feel pretty good right about now, I'm happy to say. "Smug" is not a word my mom would be proud to hear me choose when describing myself, but it's right on. Look, I've made some pretty bad decisions (New York, New York), but I've made some good ones, too—why not own it?

I was playing basketball today with some guys from my master's program. We're making friends with one another, but we also all feel too old and too cool to *try* to make friends. It's pretty funny, sort of like a "What's up, bro? Want to shoot hoops? I don't give a shit either way, just so you know."

But a lot of us did want to play, as it turned out. We played for about an hour, and then one by one, people said they had to go, because they had to get to their jobs at the library, or the student center, or the gym.

"What about you, dude?" one guy, Jake, asked me. "Do you work?"

"Not now," I said, "but I worked as a nanny until last month."

Well, that stopped everyone in their Air Jordans.

"Seriously?"

"A nanny?"

"Like, a *manny*?"

"Yep," I said. "It was pretty cool. I might do it again over the summer if I can't get the summer school courses I want."

"You didn't tell chicks what you did, right?"

I shrugged. "If they asked. But most of the women I hung out with worked there, too. The family I worked for had a big staff."

This being Los Angeles, they knew what I meant. I'd worked for a celebrity, and I couldn't tell them who.

"I still don't get it, dude," another guy, Aaron, said. "I don't know anyone else who's a manny. Why didn't you work security or something? You're big enough."

"I like working with kids," I said. "And nannies make bank. While you assholes are all working tonight, I'll be free to study. Then I'm going to chill out in Hawaii for a while over Christmas."

"Yeah, but don't you have to change diapers and crap like that?" Jake asked.

"*That's* not a pickup line I'd use on a woman, Jake." I smiled.

"You didn't answer the question," he said.

"I can't say much," I said, "but I can tell you I still hang out with the kid I watched, just for fun. In fact, we'll be courtside at the Lakers game next week."

That shut them right up. It was a bit of a white lie, but even if we didn't have tickets for the game, I'd still be hanging out with Chase that night. He's a good kid, and I'm grateful to him. He showed me what I want to do with my life. And the job with him is helping me do it without handing out towels at a gym. All good things.

TRACY

I had a very odd encounter at the park today.

Colin and I had a lovely morning together. We went to his music lesson, then out for a spot of lunch, and then to the park to burn off some of his extra energy before his nap. The weather is gorgeous right now in Los Angeles. Not too hot, for a change.

I was pushing Colin in the swing when someone called my name, and I looked up to see an old friend, Meredith. Meredith and I had become fast friends when I moved to the States because, like me, she was a nanny transplant from London. We bonded over our love for the work.

Over time, we'd lost touch, and I heard she'd gotten married to some bigwig. Not a celebrity, but some big financier or some such. I was happy for her. Surprised, but happy.

We embraced and she introduced me to the adorable little cherub on her hip, Maisy.

"So you're still nannying, then?" I asked.

"Oh no!" she said. "This is my baby."

I'm not sure exactly why I was so taken aback, but I was. I studied the little girl's features. She did, in fact, have her mother's blue eyes, and soft blond ringlets. In fact, she was the spitting image of Meredith.

"Of course!" I said. "I can see the resemblance. How strange it must be to have another being who looks so much like you."

"'Strange' is one word for it," she said good-naturedly. "It feels sort of . . . I dunno, *magical*, I suppose. I can't describe it—you'd think I'd know all about what it means to be a mum since I've taken care of so many kids. But I didn't have a clue having your own is so different. I wouldn't have believed that when I was just a nanny."

"Mmm," I said, because I wasn't quite certain what I should say. What did she mean, "just a nanny"?

Meredith must have sensed my discomfort, because she changed the subject. "And how are you, darling? Working for a nice family now?"

"Oh yes," I said. "They're lovely."

"That's great to hear!" Meredith said. I sensed some edge to her voice, like she was patting me on the back for a life well done. I turned the conversation to music classes and Gymboree programs I preferred for Colin. Then Colin got a bit fussy, and I knew it was time for his nap. I pulled him from the swing and grabbed the diaper bag.

"Tracy," Meredith said in a hesitant voice, "you know, if anything changes with the family you're working for, anything at all, I'd love to have you come work with us."

Work with her? She meant *for* her, of course. So the former nanny hires a nanny. I suppose I should have felt flattered—she knew firsthand what it took to be a top-notch nanny, and liked my work enough to want to hire me. But I didn't feel flattered. I felt insulted.

And why? Wasn't I always going on and on about the value of a true childcare professional's work? Didn't I believe that how I made my living was worthy? Absolutely.

Perhaps what I was really feeling was jealousy. Perhaps I wanted to be the one holding a mini-me on my hip, offering *Meredith* a job. But that ship had sailed. I had pushed it away, and then watched it go. And I knew, in my heart of hearts, that it was the right decision for me to have made. It was. I'm sure of it. Of course it was. *The lady doth protest too much, methinks.*

LAURA

I was positively swarmed after my speech. It was awesome, especially considering it was my very first public speaking gig and how nervous I was.

The talk was the first of a lecture series on parenting. I didn't think anyone would come. I expected a throng of critics shouting, "She doesn't even have kids!" But that's exactly how I knew my advice was good: I had objectivity. I was (imperious throat-clearing here) a *professional*.

After I got my bachelor's degree (which took no time at all once I stopped working), I wrote a few blogs, sharing tips and secrets I learned from nannying. Pretty quickly, I had a large following, and my social media–crazy friend Janeese told me I needed to start marketing the hell out of myself. I started tweeting. I started making YouTube videos. And I started offering a lecture series.

Who knew parents would want to hear what I had to say?

Who knew how great it felt to be your own boss?

Best of all, I also started a nanny support group. All the placement agencies send distraught nannies my way, and I clean them right up. Annoyed that your boss keeps coming on to you? Let's talk. Frustrated that the parents never deny their kids anything? Come to me; we'll talk. Having a hard time telling your boss what you need? Go figure—that happens to be my specialty!

Starting your own business isn't exactly a cakewalk. I've been nervous about money, nervous about whether it would all come together or not. But so far (knock on wood), so good. And I've got backups.

I went to a job interview yesterday, just in case my lecture series bombed. I'm the kind of girl who likes a little insurance. It wasn't a nanny interview; it was for a job in marketing.

"You've been a nanny for years," the super-boring bald guy who interviewed me began. "How does that qualify you for a job in marketing and communications?"

"I *get* people," I said, and realized it was true. "I know what approach will work with some people and not with others. I understand, from working with so many types of parents, what makes different people tick."

Boring bald guy nodded. *This is a marketing agency!* I thought. *Where's hipster guy? Where's the foosball table?*

"Go on," he prompted.

"I'm a great communicator," I said, having fun with it. "In my last job, I had to have very hard, very sensitive conversations with my boss, and that was made easier by my perceiving what it was she wanted and needed to hear. I know how to spin a message."

"Hmm, go on," bald guy said again.

"I'm a consummate professional." This was the one I was perhaps most proud of, truth be told. "I don't lose my cool. I can be the grown-up among grown-ups."

That made him laugh. "Have you had to do that much in your job? Parent grown-ups?"

"At times," I said. "But one of my other qualities is discretion, you see, so I can't say much more."

He laughed harder, asked me to send him a writing sample, and sent me on my way.

Maybe I'll take the job if I get it, but probably not. I feel like I have options, and the best among them so far is to see if I can grow a business. Because at the end of the day, I became a nanny because I love children. I adore them. I've always seen myself working with them, one way or another. And if

I can train other nannies, and parents, how to work with the children in their lives, that might just be the perfect thing.

And if it isn't, I'm not afraid to walk away.

.   .   .

We look upon the stories of Kirsten, Jeremy, Tracy, and Laura with great affection. Despite what it may seem like, not one of these nannies is unsuccessful. Kirsten is a newer version of herself and, years from now, we can't wait to see where she's landed. Perhaps she'll be a career nanny, like Tracy. Or perhaps she'll be one of the nannies who is successful at having a full personal life while also holding down a celebrity nanny position.

Jeremy was a bit ahead of the game to begin with. Though new to the nanny business, he brought significant life experience that served him well in his job. He has his eye on the ball, doesn't suffer fools, and, though a bit naïve at first, he is a quick learner. How much of his path is made easier by his gender? Our view is that his sex works both for him and against him. He has to put up with unfair stereotypes of male nannies. But he also benefits from unfair stereotypes of female nannies.

And Tracy. Oh, dear Tracy! We hesitate to judge Tracy too much. We think her decision to turn away from love was an unfortunate one, but, then again, we are nothing if not romantics. There are other jobs, but will there ever be another

Tom for her? Perhaps so. Perhaps she needed to love and lose Tom in order to be ready to let someone in. Or perhaps she's content and happy in the role she plays, and needs very little in the way of romance herself. But even Mary Poppins had a flirtation with a chimney sweep, and we can't help but hope for just a bit more spice in Tracy's life.

Laura is probably the nearest to our hearts. Laura is the nanny we see most frequently: eager, ambitious, smart, energetic—and totally unprepared for the world of Nannywood. Laura is forced to grow up, to see the world not as she wants it to be, but as it is. She must buck up and deal with it, and find her own path and her own voice. Her self-worth is challenged, and reclaimed. Her comfort with risk is tested, and conquered. We may all in fact be working for Laura someday, and what a fine boss she'd be.

Of course, we've really only told you half the story here. You've seen this insane industry from the point of view of the nanny, but something is missing, is it not? What about those mums and dads who are overworked and trying their best? They have their own frustrations with their nannies, who are often younger and less experienced in the ways of the world, and sometimes quite entitled. Mum and dad are sincerely trying to do right by their kids, just as they are trying to keep a grip in a world that would push them off the ledge at the slightest provocation. That can't be easy. And so, what of these mums and dads? Where are their stories?

Ah, dear readers. Stay tuned.

ACKNOWLEDGMENTS

• • • • • • • • • • • • • • • • • • • •

From us both, thanks go to the following people:

- All the nannies who gave their time and stories for this book.
- All the families we have both worked with over the years.
- Jenna Free and everyone at Girl Friday Productions.
- Paul Barrett for the best cover ever.
- Sarah Michelle Gellar for the Foreword.
- Everyone who wrote testimonials, including Emma Jenner, Irma Blanco, Suzy Shuster, Rich Eisen, Celia Walden, Marissa Devins, Michelle LaRowe, and Lindsay Heller.

From Stella, thanks go to:

- Mike and Mason, my greatest achievements.
- Julie Swales, with love and gratitude.

From Julie, thanks go to:

- My two Jacks: Jack Lippman, with whom I have worked for 21 years, and Jack Grapes, with whom I have studied writing for 10 years.
- Stella Reid, with love and gratitude.

And to our favorite nannies of all:

- Mary Poppins
- Maria Rainer (who was the future Maria von Trapp)
- Nanny McPhee
- Aibileen Clark
- Mrs. Doubtfire
- And, of course, Jane Eyre

CPSIA information can be obtained
at www.ICGtesting.com
Printed in the USA
LVOW13s0004290118
564398LV00008B/92/P